With
love from
Ukraine

♡

Y. Klopotenko

ЄВГЕН КЛОПОТЕНКО

ЗВАБЛЕННЯ ЇЖЕЮ З УКРАЇНСЬКИМ СМАКОМ

#книголав/Київ/2020

IEVGEN KLOPOTENKO

UKRAINIAN CUISINE
IN 70 DISHES

*TRANSLATED FROM UKRAINIAN
BY IAROSLAVA STRIKHA*

#knigolove/Kyiv/2023

УДК 641.55(=161.2)(083.12)=111
К 57

Popular edition

Klopotenko, Ievgen.

К 57   Ukrainian Cuisine in 70 Dishes / Ievgen Klopotenko; translated from Ukrainian by Iaroslava Strikha. – Kyiv: Knigolove, 2023. – 176 p.

ISBN 978–617–7820–85–6

What are the first dishes that come to mind when you hear the words "Ukrainian cuisine"? Is it borscht or dumplings? You know what else would have come to mind if you were a 19th-century Ukrainian? Shpundra, teteria, kvasha and many other dishes. What is the authentic Ukrainian cuisine, and which forgotten dishes deserve a revival? Ievgen Klopotenko is answering these questions in his new book. He has spent several years exploring Ukrainian cookbooks from different eras, travelling across Ukraine and consulting with historians to develop his own vision of the Ukrainian cuisine. This book compiles 70 recipes that could bridge the gap between the Ukrainian culinary past and the present. You will rediscover the long forgotten Ukrainian dishes with a contemporary twist and new takes on old favorites. We guarantee that you will fall in love with these dishes and will be inspired to explore Ukraine's culinary diversity with us.

УДК 641.55(=161.2)(083.12)=111

Editorial group: *Oleksii Tatianchenko, Hanna Li, Iryna Rudnievska, Yevheniia Ieskova, Olena Liubenko, Olena Parkhomets*
Food styling by *Iryna Rudnievska, Oleksii Tatianchenko*
Photography by *Yuliia Minytska, Yuliia Hamova, Mykola Borysenko*
Design by *Valeriia Likhachova*
Cover design by *Maryna Fudashkina*
Proofreading by *Dariia Puhach*
Project curator: *Oleksandra Fidkevych*

The English-language edition team:
Translator: *Iaroslava Strikha*
Consulting editor: *Oleksandra Povoroznyk*
Layout designer: *Olha Fesenko*
Executive editor: *Daryna Vazhynska*
Editor in chief: *Zhanna Kapshuk*
Responsible editor: *Dmytro Oskolkov*

Signed to print 02.11.2023. Format 84×108/16. Conventional printed sheet 18,48.
Print run 1500 copies. Order. № 2509.

Knigolove LLC, 31A Pravda Avenue, Kyiv, 04108. Publisher's license № 7521 of 29.11.2021.
knigolove.ua • facebook.com/knygolove • instagram.com/knygolove • sayhello@knigolove.ua

Printed by Printing house "From A to Z" LLC. 38/40 Kolektorna Str., Kyiv, 02121.
Publisher's license № 1844. www.fromatoz.ua

ISBN 978–617–7820–85–6

IT'S TIME TO DISCOVER UKRAINIAN CUISINE. IT'S MORE THAN WORTH THE EFFORT

CONTENTS

INTRODUCTION

Strange as it may sound, the majority of present-day Ukrainians are plagued by negative stereotypes about their own cuisine. They might know borscht and dumplings, but anything beyond that is a mystery to them. I, too, used to belong to that majority. That is all due to our history. The Soviet Union did its best to wipe out not only the Ukrainian cuisine but also the very Ukrainian worldview. The moment I realized that, I dove into research. I was stunned by the magnificence of the Ukrainian dishes that our ancestors used to cook hundreds of years ago. With each bite, you feel the connection to your history. I began to tell this to Ukrainians to help them see that the love for all things Ukrainian was alive and well in our hearts. Some keep it in the dark, chained and bound; in some, the love has just awakened, so it's still a little groggy and confused from the sleep. Some though have let their love flow freely, so it grew, blossomed and strengthened, becoming their inspiration and protection.

If you love your roots, you are never alone. You know what you live for, and you know that others just like you are always at arm's length. You know where you fit in, and you have support. Oh, and it's simply a cool thing to do: to choose to love all things Ukrainian. If you choose to love, everything you do is steeped in that feeling, empowering you to create something beautiful.

Now I'd like to share my love for all things Ukrainian with the whole wide world. One could do that through our history, or our writers and their biographies, or through the thrilling Ukrainian music. Me, I will do it through Ukrainian cuisine. The national cuisine upholds an emotional connection with the country. This is the time to ask the question: what is Ukrainian cuisine?

Everybody thinks that Ukrainian cuisine is all about borscht and dumplings... and that's about it. They couldn't be more wrong. It took me approximately four years, about a hundred cookbooks from various eras, a trip across the entire country and countless consultations with historians to form my own understanding and sense of the Ukrainian cuisine. And here's what I've got to tell you.

First, sugar beet, home-pressed sunflower oil and beetroot kvass are the three products that are a part of our very DNA. Can you imagine the rich sweet taste of a baked sugar beet? Right, it's as if God kissed you on the mouth.

8

Second, Ukrainian cuisine is much more versatile than you might imagine. We know barely 15% of it. It's funny, really, that we have wasted so many years without making an effort to discover it. We had a very superficial idea of it, when in reality, Ukrainian cuisine is much deeper, more serious and less stereotypical than we might believe. It may surprise you. Cook any five dishes from this book, and you will feel your heart pulse with joy and excitement. This stuff is addictive. It's like meeting a woman that you want to drown in. She's slightly older and utterly magical. Endowed with deep wisdom and electric energy, she makes you feel like a slightly better version of yourself even if she's not doing anything in particular.

Ukrainian cuisine is a great historical record of the Ukrainian past and present. Some dishes were even adopted from other cultures: you will find several such recipes on the pages of this book. They won't leave your heart cold, I promise. Not a single dish here will leave your heart cold.

This is Ukrainian cuisine for you. It's delicious, but that's not the only reason why it's important. Ukrainian cuisine will help you understand Ukrainians as a nation. It's like taking a trip, only without getting on a plane or buying museum tickets. Cook it and try it, and you'll see it for yourself. Each country's cuisine embodies its culture and values, essentially presenting the nation's culinary portrait. This book is not just a collection of 70 recipes: these are 70 histories of the nation that has suffered centuries of persecution. Despite all that, my nation managed to preserve its identity and independence, but it's only just now learning to be proud of itself. To be proud of its language, its history, and its cuisine.

Read, listen, cook, feel Ukrainian. This is why I created this book: to teach everybody to love Ukraine through food.

**With Ukraine in my heart and on my tongue,
Ievgen Klopotenko**

DISCOVER UKRAINIAN INGREDIENTS

Ukrainian ingredients are cool, even if Ukrainians themselves don't necessarily realize how lucky they are. They take it all for granted. Yes, other countries may have similar ingredients, but their Ukrainian version is quite unique. I'm now teaching my compatriots to recognize their vibrant and rich taste. How? This is what I've been telling them:

"When you are buying carrots, don't think that it's just a boring and humble thing that you chuck into a broth and then discard without a second thought. No, no, no. No product deserves that. When you are at the market, pick up that carrot. Say hello to it (silently). Say, 'Hello, carrot. Aren't you gorgeous?' Imagine that this is the best carrot you've seen in your life. While the carrot probably won't answer you, that thought process creates the right mindset. Imagine its taste. Sweet, crunchy, juicy. Imagine how you'd like to cook it. With an orange? With rosemary? Would you like it caramelized? Show an interest in it. Imagine how much effort went into growing that carrot: not just human effort either, but of nature as a whole. Isn't it a miracle? You sow seeds, and then the sun, the rain and the soil all contribute to growing something delicious beyond all imagination.

This is true not only of carrots but of any product at all. A beetroot? Enough with boiling it, I'm begging you. Roast it. Eat it raw, savoring its honey sweetness. Or take earth apples, for example. At a farmer's market, you wouldn't touch this weird alien with a ten-foot pole. Pause. Buy it, bring it home, slice it, roast it and eat it with parsley, lemon and mustard. Try fragrant home-pressed oils and learn to love their mouth-watering aroma."

I want Ukrainians to respect the fruit of their soil. Me, I'm bubbling with excitement whenever I hit the farmer's market. It's like falling in love. Everything is so fragrant, so fresh, so precious. My heart feels ready to burst out of my chest. I feel dizzy. I love this feeling. I love imagining how I'd wash these vegetables, slice them, cook them, eat them...

I feel grateful because Ukrainian vegetables, fruit and other foods are some of the most delicious in the world. Ukrainians are beyond lucky to have them within easy reach.

MEAT

Historically, meat was a rare treat for Ukrainians. First, observant Orthodox Christians in Ukraine used to spend approximately six months out of twelve fasting. Second, only the wealthiest were rich enough to regularly feast on meat. All the others had their share of meat only on major holidays. Therefore, it is assumed that up until the mid-20th century, Ukrainians had a predominantly plant-based diet. That said, they loved meat a lot and jumped at every opportunity to savor some.

What do we see now? Finally having meat aplenty, Ukrainians became ardent meat-eaters. We have it for breakfast, lunch and dinner, and get anxious whenever our meat level drops critically. As if making up for past centuries, we can even devour several meat dishes during one meal. To be perfectly blunt, we aren't content unless we have some sort of meat in the fridge. It's usually the meat of domesticated animals: poultry, beef and pork are our favorites, hands down.

We usually roast meat. Note that we have inherited this technology from our ancestors, who cooked everything in the oven. Wow, I got chills just from thinking about this connection that transcends the boundaries of time and space.

By the way, ground meat is not a typical or traditional method of processing meat for Ukrainians. We used to finely dice or chop meat into the kind of small pieces you'd see in meat rolls or homemade sausages.

That might surprise you, but the idea that Ukrainians traditionally preferred very fatty meat dishes is wrong. In reality, we always used to take good care of our bodies, and never overdid it with the fat. This changed in Soviet times, when fat was the only available source of lasting energy, given that people couldn't afford much food.

So let us leave our stereotypes behind, open the chapter with meat dishes, and enjoy the delicious authentic tastes.

#1 HRECHANYKY (BUCKWHEAT PATTIES) WITH TOMATO SAUCE

45 MINUTES   **SERVES 6**

INGREDIENTS:

- 300 G / 10 OZ. GROUND CHICKEN
- 125 G / 1 CUP BUCKWHEAT GRITS
- 50 G / 1¾ OZ. PORK FAT / FATTY BACON
- 250 ML / 1 CUP WATER
- 2 EGGS
- ½ TSP. SALT
- ⅓ TSP. GROUND BLACK PEPPER
- 3-4 TBSP. SEMOLINA FOR COATING
- 3-4 TBSP. VEGETABLE OIL

FOR THE SAUCE:

- 2-3 TBSP. TOMATO PASTE
- 200 ML / ¾ CUP PLUS 2 TBSP. WATER
- 3-4 GARLIC CLOVES
- ½ CHILI PEPPER
- 1 APPLE
- 1 TSP. INSTANT COFFEE
- A PINCH OF SUGAR
- A PINCH OF SALT

1. Preheat oven to 180°C / 350°F degrees.

2. Cover the buckwheat grits with water, add a pinch of salt, and cook for 15 minutes until ready. Leave them to cool.

3. Add ground chicken, finely diced pork fat or fatty bacon, salt and pepper. Mix the ingredients well, and form patties.

4. Coat the patties with semolina and place them on an oiled roasting pan. Roast for 15–20 minutes.

5. **For the sauce**, mix tomato paste with water and a coarsely grated apple. Add slices of chili pepper, salt and sugar, and sauté for 2–3 minutes. Just before removing the sauce from heat, add instant coffee.

6. Serve the buckwheat patties with hot tomato sauce.

#2 ROASTED PORK FAT IN CHAMOMILE

45 MINUTES | **SERVES 4**

INGREDIENTS:

· 0.5 KG / 1 LB. PORK FAT

· 1 TBSP. DRIED CHAMOMILE
  FLOWERS

· SALT

1. Preheat oven to 180°C / 350°F degrees.

2. Rub pork fat with a generous amount of salt (if unsalted) and dried chamomile flowers.

3. Roast on a baking paper-lined tray for 35–40 minutes.

4. Cool to room temperature and serve thinly sliced.

#3 SHPUNDRY (BEETROOT AND PORK STEW)

2 HOURS   SERVES 4

INGREDIENTS:

· 500 G / 1 LB. PORK NECK OR
  RIBS

· 1-2 BEETROOTS

· 1 TBSP. VINEGAR

· 2 ONIONS

· 1 TSP. SWEET MUSTARD

· 3 CLOVES GARLIC

· 1 TBSP. VEGETABLE OIL

· 40 G / 2½ TBSP. UNSALTED
  BUTTER

· 2 TBSP. ALL-PURPOSE FLOUR

· 1-2 TBSP. HORSERADISH

· 2-4 TBSP. SOUR CREAM

· 3-5 SPRIGS OF THYME
  (OPTIONAL)

· SALT, PEPPER

1. Preheat oven to 180°C / 350°F degrees.

2. Cut the meat, season with salt and pepper to taste. Rub it with sweet mustard and sprinkle with oil. Place it on a tray with one onion sliced into thin half circles. Roast for 40 minutes.

3. When cooked, separate the meat from the ribs, or slice the pork neck into bite-sized pieces.

4. Wash the beetroot well and place it in the oven. It's best to choose smaller beets and roast the meat and the beetroots simultaneously.

5. Slice the cooked beetroot into half circles, add vinegar and water until the beets are completely covered. Leave to marinate for 40 minutes.

6. Fry a finely chopped onion in butter in a large pan, add the meat and marinated beetroots. Add half a cup of water, and let it stew for 5 minutes.

7. Add flour, salt and pepper to taste.

8. Serve *shpundry* with grated white horseradish and sour cream. You can also add fresh thyme leaves.

#4 POLTAVA HALUSHKY (DUMPLINGS) WITH SOUR CHERRIES AND MEAT

45 MINUTES

SERVES 6

INGREDIENTS:

· 400 G / 3½ CUPS ALL-PURPOSE FLOUR
· 250 ML / 1 CUP KEFIR (FERMENTED MILK DRINK, CAN BE SUBSTITUTED WITH THIN PLAIN YOGHURT)
· 1 EGG
· ½ TSP. SALT
· ½ TSP. BAKING SODA
· 500 G / 1 LB. GROUND-MEAT MIX
· 1 TBSP. SUGAR

FOR THE SAUCE:

· 400 G / 1 LB. FROZEN SOUR CHERRIES
· ½ TSP. GROUND CORIANDER SEEDS
· GROUND BLACK PEPPER
· ½ CUP SOUR CREAM
· 2-3 TBSP. VEGETABLE OIL

1. Prepare the dough for *halushky*. Mix flour, kefir, eggs, salt and baking soda in a bowl. Knead the dough until it is soft and not sticky.

2. Pinch off small pieces of dough and toss them into boiling salted water. Cook for 2 minutes, then remove *halushky* with a skimmer. Sprinkle the cooked *halushky* with oil so that they won't stick together. Cover with a towel and leave in a warm place to ensure that they don't cool before serving.

3. **Prepare the sauce.** Fry minced meat in a pan with a small sprinkling of oil. Season with salt, ground coriander and pepper to taste.

4. 5 minutes before the meat is ready, add defrosted, pitted sour cherries with juice.

5. Mix *halushky* with fried meat and cherries in a large bowl. Serve hot with sour cream.

KRUCHENYKY (MEAT ROLLS)

45 MINUTES | **SERVES 2**

INGREDIENTS:

· 250 G / 0.5 LB. PORK LOIN

· 100 G / 3½ OZ. PORK FAT OR

 FATTY BACON

· 1 CLOVE GARLIC

· A PINCH OF THYME

· 10-12 SPRIGS OF FRESH DILL

· 50 G / ⅓ CUP FLOUR

· 50 G / ¼ CUP SEMOLINA

· 2-3 TBSP. VEGETABLE OIL

· 1 EGG

· SALT, PEPPER

1. Preheat oven to 180°C / 350°F degrees.

2. Cut the pork loin into portion-sized pieces. Cover with plastic wrap and pound each piece until tender. Rub it with salt and pepper.

3. Mix small pieces of pork fat or fatty bacon with finely chopped garlic and dill. Add thyme and blend in a food processor until smooth.

4. Form the fat-and-herbs mass into logs, place each in the center of a pork loin piece, leaving room on the sides, then roll up. Secure each roll with a toothpick.

5. On to the two-step coating process. Coat each meat roll in flour, then dip into egg wash, and then sprinkle with semolina.

6. Place the rolls on a hot oiled pan and fry for several minutes until golden brown on all sides.

7. Move the rolls to a roasting tray lined with baking paper and roast for 15 minutes.

#6 DUCK WITH BANOSH (CORNMEAL PORRIDGE)

4 HOURS

SERVES 4-6

INGREDIENTS:

· 1 DUCK

· 100 G / ¾ CUP CORNMEAL

· 100 ML / 7 TBSP. HEAVY CREAM

· 100 ML / 7 TBSP. MILK

· 100 ML / 7 TBSP. WATER

· 1 ONION

· 1 CARROT

· 1 BELL PEPPER

· 2-3 CLOVES GARLIC

· 5 SPRIGS OF THYME

· ⅓ CHILI PEPPER

· 2-3 TBSP. VEGETABLE OIL

· JUICE AND ZEST OF 1 LEMON

· SALT, PEPPER

1. Preheat oven to 180°C / 350°F degrees.

2. **Prepare the banosh.** Mix cream, milk and water in a heavy saucepan, bring to a boil and cook for 3-5 minutes, whisking constantly.

3. **Vegetables.** Dice an onion, a carrot and a bell pepper. Fry them in an oiled pan until golden brown.

4. Add the vegetables to the cornmeal and mix well.

5. Rub the **duck** with salt and pepper (inside and out), sprinkle with lemon zest and juice and oil. Stuff crushed garlic cloves, sprigs of thyme and thin slices of a hot chili pepper inside the duck. Leave it to marinate for 1.5-2 hours.

6. Fill the duck with vegetable banosh and close the skin with toothpicks or kitchen twine.

7. Bake for 1.5 hours. Now and again baste the duck with its juices from the tray.

8. Serve the duck with banosh stuffing while still hot.

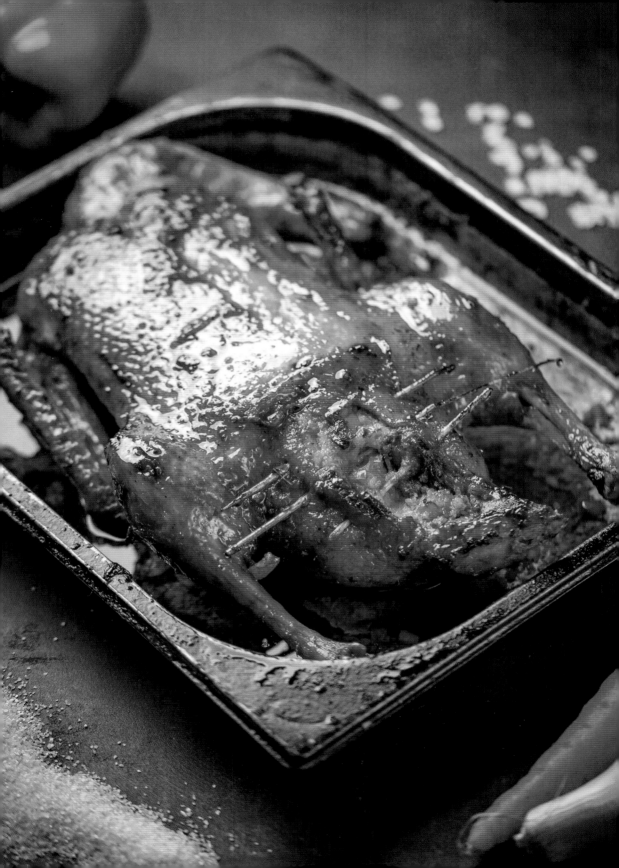

DRAHLI (ASPIC)

3 HOURS | **SERVES 4**

INGREDIENTS:

· 500 G / 1 LB. LEAN PORK

· 2 LITERS / 8 CUPS WATER

· 30 G / 1 OZ. UNFLAVORED

  GELATIN POWDER

· 2-3 CLOVES GARLIC

· 3-4 ALLSPICE BERRIES

· 2-3 BAY LEAVES

FOR THE SAUCE:

· 2 CLOVES GARLIC

· ¼ TSP. BLACK PEPPER

· 2 TSP. WHITE HORSERADISH

1. Cut lean pork into bite-sized chunks, put into a saucepan, cover with water and bring to a boil. After cooking for 2–3 minutes, drain the water and wash the meat well.

2. Add new clean water, combine with crushed garlic, allspice and bay leaf, and cook over low heat for 1 hour. Add salt to taste.

3. Remove the meat, shred and place into portion-sized bowls.

4. Dissolve the previously soaked gelatin in the hot broth and pour into the bowls over the meat. After the broth cools, put the bowls in the fridge and leave for 2–3 hours for the aspic to set.

5. For the sauce, mix crushed garlic with black pepper and white horseradish. Serve the aspic with the hot sauce.

#8

ZINKIV SAUSAGE

4 HOURS   SERVES 6-8

INGREDIENTS:

· 2 KG / 4½ LB. LEAN PORK

  SHOULDER

· 1 TBSP. SALT

· 1 TBSP. FRESHLY GROUND

  BLACK PEPPER OR MIXED

  PEPPERS

· 3 METERS PORK INTESTINES

· 3 HEADS GARLIC

· 250 ML / 1 CUP ICE-COLD

  WATER

· 500 ML / 2 CUPS FRESH PIG'S

  BLOOD (YOU CAN PROBABLY

  GET IT FROM YOUR BUTCHER

  OR ASK AROUND AT A MEAT

  MARKET)

1. Preheat oven to 160°C / 325°F degrees.

2. Cut the meat into approximately 0.5 to 1-inch (1–2 cm) cubes and put in a bowl.

3. Season with salt, freshly ground pepper and crushed garlic. Carefully mix the ingredients for 10–15 minutes until the sausage mixture becomes denser.

4. Add ice-cold water and mix thoroughly once again until the meat absorbs all liquid.

5. Soak and rinse pork intestines. You can also get artificial sausage casings, but I prefer the natural hog casing (you can order intestines from a reputable butcher or at the farmer's market).

6. Cut the intestines into 40–60 cm / 15–25 inch segments and fill them with the sausage blend using a sausage stuffer. Make sure you fill the casing as tightly as possible and close the ends with kitchen twine.

7. Rub the sausages with blood roast for 3 hours. In the early stages, remove the sausage from the oven every 20 minutes and rub with blood on both sides with a pastry brush. To make sure that the sausage turns the nice dark shade and doesn't dry out, you'll need to repeat this process 5–6 times.

8. Towards the end of the cooking time, you can place a beech or alder wood chip in a bowl, light it and put it in the oven to give the sausage a nice smoke-cured taste.

9. Serve the sausage fully cooled.

#9
VERESHCHAKA (KVASS-COOKED RIBS)

 |

1 HOUR 20 MINUTES

SERVES 4

INGREDIENTS:

· 600-800 G / 1.3-1.7 LB. PORK RIBS

· 200 ML / SCANT 1 CUP BEETROOT
  KVASS (SEE THE RECIPE ON P. 165)

· 200 ML / SCANT 1 CUP WHEAT
  KVASS (YOU CAN FIND KVASS
  IN EASTERN EUROPEAN
  GROCERY STORES OR ONLINE)

· 2 SPRIGS THYME

· 1/2 TBSP. SUGAR

· 2-3 CLOVES GARLIC

· 50 G / 3½ TBSP. UNSALTED
  BUTTER

· 1 TBSP. FLOUR

· 2-3 TBSP. VEGETABLE OIL

· SALT, PEPPER

1. Preheat oven to 180°C / 350°F degrees.

2. Remove membranes and extra fat from the ribs. Cut into servings of 1–2 segments.

3. Rub the ribs with salt, pepper and crushed garlic.

4. Fry on a frying pan with a small dollop of vegetable oil until a golden brown crust forms on all sides.

5. Move the ribs to a deep roasting tray and add two kinds of kvass: beetroot and wheat. Roast for 45–50 minutes.

6. Once ready, remove the ribs from the tray and serve hot.

7. Meanwhile, prepare the sauce: pour the leftover juices from the roasting pan into a saucepan and reduce for 20 minutes.

8. Mix softened butter with flour until smooth. Add the mixture to the saucepan, season with sugar, salt and pepper to taste to make sure that the sauce caramelizes and glazes. Keep whisking until the sauce thickens smoothly.

9. Serve with a generous helping of the sauce.

#10 CHEBUREKY (CRIMEAN TATAR TURNOVER)

1 HOUR   SERVES 4-6

INGREDIENTS:

· 600 G / 5 SCANT CUPS ALL-PURPOSE FLOUR

· 250 ML / 1 CUP WATER

· 1 TSP. SALT

· 1 TSP. SUGAR

· 1 TSP. VINEGAR

· 1 TSP. VEGETABLE OIL

FOR THE FILLING:

· 800 G / 1.7 LB. GROUND BEEF

· 1 LARGE ONION

· 4-5 CLOVES GARLIC

· 1 TBSP. CUMIN

· 200 ML / ¾ CUP PLUS 2 TBSP. COLD WATER

· SALT, PEPPER

· FRYING OIL

1. **For the dough,** add salt, sugar, vinegar, and warm water (50°C / 120°F) to sifted flour. Knead the dough until stretchy and elastic, then cover with plastic wrap. Leave it to rest for 30 minutes in the fridge.

2. **For the filling,** finely dice the onion with a sharp knife and mix with ground beef and crushed garlic. Season with salt, pepper and cumin to taste. Add very cold water and stir very well to make the filling juicier.

3. Separate the dough into 12-15 equal portions and roll out each until thin. Brush the edges with a little bit of water to make them stickier. Place the filling over one half of the dough, then fold the other half to cover the filling and press down the edge with a fork to give it the desired wavy texture.

4. Fry *chebureky* in oil on a hot frying pan until both sides are golden brown.

5. Serve hot right from the pan.

#11

PORK STEW

2 HOURS | **SERVES 4-6**

INGREDIENTS:

- 800 G / 1.7 LB. FATTY PORK (NECK)
- ¼ CELERY ROOT
- 6-8 POTATOES
- 3-4 TBSP. VEGETABLE OIL
- 150 G / 5 OZ. PORK FAT
- 1-2 ONIONS
- 1 CARROT
- 1 GARLIC
- 100 ML / 7 TBSP. DRY RED WINE
- 1-2 TBSP. TOMATO PASTE
- 3-5 SPRIGS OF PARSLEY FOR DECORATION
- SALT, PEPPER

1. Preheat oven to 180°C / 350°F degrees.

2. Fry pieces of meat in a hot oiled skillet until golden brown.

3. In a frying pan, render the pork fat and fry the finely chopped onions, carrot and celery with the fat. Add crushed cloves of garlic. Cook everything together until soft, then add to the skillet with the meat.

4. Peel potatoes and chop them into small pieces. Add to the skillet with salt, pepper and ½ liter / 2 cups water. Bake for 40 minutes.

5. Dissolve the tomato paste in wine and pour it into the skillet. Put it back into the oven and cook for 30–40 more minutes until ready.

6. Serve the pork stew hot. Optionally, you can garnish the stew with finely chopped green parsley.

FISH

A nation is formed by its language and cuisine. That's 2/3 of the formula for success. Whenever we travel abroad, we try to learn a couple of words in a local language and find out what the locals eat. Our introduction to a new culture usually begins with these two factors. Therefore, it comes as no surprise that I only started to feel fully Ukrainian after I began to study the national cuisine. I grew up in Ukraine and I love my country, but I always felt like something was missing, as if our relationship wasn't deep enough. After I found out that, say, our ancestors in Ukraine used to stew pork ribs in kvass, my eyes opened. I realized that, up to that day, the list of authentic Ukrainian dishes that I had tried was limited to borscht and banosh. I knew more about Italian cuisine than about my own culture.

That realization had changed everything. I began to seek out, cook and eat Ukrainian dishes. Each new flavor made my connection with Ukraine grow stronger. A couple dozen dishes, and we are no longer strangers. My knowledge about the national cuisine has unblocked our connection.

That knowledge gave me an instinctual understanding of Ukraine. I dug deeper and formed my own understanding of what it means to be Ukrainian. In my search for Ukrainian national cuisine, I ended up finding myself. It was as if a chest with a portal to a different time opened in front of me. That chest stores history and love for my country and people. That crucial chest had been hidden from me for so long that, having finally found it, I wanted to show its contents to other Ukrainians. I wanted to develop, protect and promote Ukrainian cuisine. I loved the Ukrainian part of my identity more than ever, and that has changed how I viewed others. I realized that they didn't care about certain things only because they didn't have the information that I've found. They didn't understand who they were, and they didn't have the knowledge of history that could unite them.

Food, it seems, has brought me to the authentic Ukrainian world. Not only is it a land of many wonders; most crucially, it has a future. In that future, Ukrainians are a united, strong, independent and developed nation. Every Ukrainian can access that world. All you need is an entrance ticket: a connection to your roots, an understanding of and emotional investment in your history. Can a person not of Ukrainian heritage understand that world? Sure, through Ukrainian history and cuisine, which can bring one as close to Ukrainian culture as is humanly possible without actually delving into the depths of Ukrainian national character. That understanding will be partly rational, and partly emotional because food touches the soul.

#12 SILVER CARP SALAMUR (MARINADE)

30 MINUTES | **SERVES 6**

INGREDIENTS:

· 1 SILVER CARP (700 G / 1½ LB.)

· 1 CARROT

· 1 ONION

· 1.5 TSP. SALT

· 70 ML / 4.5 TBSP. VINEGAR

FOR THE SALAMUR (MARINADE):

· 40 ML / 2½ TBSP. VINEGAR

· 3 CLOVES GARLIC

· 5-7 SPRIGS DILL

· 150 ML / ⅔ CUP VEGETABLE OIL

· 1 TSP. SALT

1. Scale the fish, remove intestines and fins. Chop off the tail and the head (they will make for a delicious fish broth). Slice the fish into 2 cm / ¾ inch-thick steaks.

2. Prepare the vegetables for the broth. Slice the onion into half-circles, and the carrot into chunks of whatever size you like. Cover the vegetables with 1½ liters / 1½ quarts of water, add salt and vinegar. Mix well and heat up. Add fish steaks, bring to a boil and cook for 10 minutes.

3. For the marinade, mix oil and vinegar in a glass bowl. Add salt, finely diced green dill, and crushed garlic. Mix well.

4. Remove fish steaks from the broth and cover with marinade. Leave to rest in the fridge for 20 minutes and serve.

#13

FRIED CARP

**2 HOURS
40 MINUTES**

SERVES 4

INGREDIENTS:

· 5-8 FRESH CARPS WITH HEADS

  ON (DEPENDING ON THE SIZE)

· 20 G / 1½ TBSP. ALL-PURPOSE

  FLOUR

· ½ LEEK

· 5 SPRIGS DILL

· 2 CLOVES GARLIC

· 300 G / 10 OZ. SOUR CREAM

  (15% FAT)

· 200 ML / ¾ CUP PLUS 2 TBSP.

  WHIPPING CREAM (33%)

· VEGETABLE OIL (FOR FRYING)

· SALT TO TASTE

1. Preheat oven to 160°C / 325°F degrees.

2. Wash and scale the carps, remove gills. Pat dry with a paper towel, sprinkle with a generous amount of salt, and leave in the fridge for 1–2 hours.

3. Roll salted carps in flour and fry in a skillet with a small glug of oil for 1 minute on each side.

4. Move the carps to an oiled roasting tray lined with slices of leeks. Pour a mixture of sour cream and cream over the fish, sprinkle with diced garlic and green dill, and bake for 20–30 minutes. Serve hot.

#14

HERB-BAKED CATFISH

 |

40 MINUTES   **SERVES 2**

INGREDIENTS:

· 1 CATFISH (300-500 G / 0.6-1.1 LB.)

· 4 TBSP. HOME-PRESSED

  VEGETABLE OIL

· 1 TSP. OREGANO

· 1 CLOVE GARLIC

· 2 TBSP. SWEET MUSTARD

· ½ TSP. DRIED ELDERBERRIES

· 3 JUNIPER BERRIES

· SALT

1. Preheat oven to 180°C / 350°F degrees.

2. Wash the catfish well, remove entrails and gills. Wash it well once again, and pat dry with a paper towel.

3. Give the catfish a generous rub of salt, then brush it with a mixture of mustard, oil, finely diced garlic, and oregano. Put crushed juniper berries into it and sprinkle it with dried elderberries.

4. Place the catfish on a baking paper-lined roasting tray and bake for 15–25 minutes, depending on the fish's size. Serve hot.

#15

BAKED CARP

1 HOUR   **SERVES 4-6**

INGREDIENTS:

· 1 CARP (APPROXIMATELY 1½ KG

  OR 3 LB.)

· 1 FENNEL ROOT

· 1 TSP. FENNEL SEEDS

· 1 LEMON

· 1 STICK CINNAMON

· 1 TBSP. SWEET MUSTARD

· 1-2 TBSP. TOMATO PASTE

  (OPTIONAL)

· 5-6 POTATOES

· VEGETABLE OIL

· SALT, PEPPER

1. Preheat oven to 180°C / 350°F degrees.

2. Wash the carp well, remove the scales, entrails and gills.

3. Pat the fish dry with a paper towel and rub it with salt and pepper. Brush it inside and out with oil. Sprinkle it with fennel seeds. Place a cinnamon stick and a fennel root, thinly sliced into half-circles, inside the fish.

4. Wash potatoes well with a sponge and cut them into large pieces. Sprinkle with salt and pepper, drizzle with oil.

5. Place the fish on an oiled roasting tray, rub with mustard and tomato paste, and sprinkle with freshly squeezed lemon juice. Put potatoes and slices of lemon around it and cook for 40–50 minutes, depending on the fish's size. Serve hot.

#16

FISH PATTIES

45 MINUTES   **SERVES 4**

INGREDIENTS:

·600-700 G / 1⅓-1½ LB. CATFISH

 FILLETS (1 SMALL CATFISH)

·100 ML / 6½ TBSP. VINEGAR

·1 ONION

·1 CARROT

·1 EGG

·1 TBSP. FLOUR

·3-4 TBSP. BREADCRUMBS

·SALT, PEPPER

1. Preheat oven to 180°C / 350°F degrees.

2. Wash the catfish well, remove entrails and gills, and cut into large steaks. Put into a saucepan, add 1 liter water, vinegar, oil and carrots cut into pieces of any size. Bring to a boil and cook for 2–3 minutes, then leave to cool in the broth.

3. Remove all bones and mince the fillet with a sharp knife. Combine with an egg and flour. Season with salt and pepper to taste. Carefully knead minced fish until all the ingredients are well-blended.

4. Form small patties of approximately 50 g / 1¾ oz, and coat them with breadcrumbs.

5. Put them on a baking paper-lined roasting tray and cook for 7–10 minutes.

6. Serve with your favorite sauce.

#17

FRIED SPRAT PATTIES

25 MINUTES   **SERVES 4**

INGREDIENTS:

· 400 G / 14 OZ. SPRATS

· 1 TBSP. VINEGAR

· 200 G / 2½ CUPS ALL-PURPOSE

  FLOUR

· 2 EGGS

· 200 ML / SCANT 1 CUP MILK

· PINCH OF SALT

· VEGETABLE OIL FOR FRYING

· ½ LEMON

· 3-4 GREEN ONION SHOOTS FOR

  SERVING

1. Remove heads and backbones of sprats, leaving just the fillets. To make the taste more intense, add salt and vinegar.

2. Prepare the batter for the patties. Mix milk, eggs and a pinch of salt with flour until it reaches the consistency of dense sour cream.

3. Place 5–6 sprat fillets on a hot oiled skillet, and pour 2–3 tbsp. of batter over it, as if you were cooking a pancake.

4. Fry the patties for 2–3 minutes on either side over low heat until golden brown.

5. Serve garnished with finely diced green or red onions and freshly pressed lemon juice.

#18

SARDINE AND VEAL STEW

1 HOUR　　**SERVES 2**

INGREDIENTS:

· 300 G / 10 OZ. VEAL

· 2 HEADS GARLIC

· 1 ONION

· 1 CARROT

· ¼ CELERY ROOT

· 2 CM / 1 INCH GINGER ROOT

· 5-6 SALTED SARDINES

· 2-3 CLOVES

· VEGETABLE OIL

· SALT, BLACK PEPPER

1. Preheat oven to 180°C / 350°F degrees.

2. Remove membranes from the veal. Cut into portion-sized slices.

3. Fry the meat, half-circular slices of onions, thick half-circles of carrots, and slices of celery of any size in a frying pan with a small dollop of oil. Add finely grated ginger to increase the flavor and taste.

4. Optionally, you can add potatoes at this stage. I decided not to add it just this time to preserve the intense vegetable flavor!

5. If your pan is oven-proof, add salt and pepper to taste, cloves and garlic heads sliced in half horizontally. Then cover with tinfoil and cook for 15–20 minutes. If the pan isn't oven-proof, move the dish to a roasting tray.

6. Prepare the sardines in advance: cut off the heads, remove the intestines and backbones. I would like to stress that the fish freshness is of the essence! It will have a huge impact on the taste of your dish.

7. Remove the tray from the oven, take off the foil and add the sardines.

8. Cover with foil again and cook for 15 more minutes.

9. Serve hot.

VEGETABLES AND MUSHROOMS

ON PARSNIP

In primary school, we used to sing a Ukrainian folk song, "A fish danced with a crayfish, and parsley danced with parsnip." The funniest thing about the song is not the total absence of logic but the fact that Ukrainians know the word "parsnip" since their earliest childhood, more or less, but don't have the foggiest idea what it actually is. If you ask a random person on the street, the majority won't be able to tell you what a parsnip looks or tastes like, and that's a shame. Have you ever tried parsnip? I did. And it's one hell of a dish.

Bittersweet and self-sufficient, it fits the Ukrainian culinary profile to a tee. Do you know what I mean? Take seafood, for example: it fits the culinary profile of Sicily. Tomatoes with mozzarella spell Italy. Thick chocolate smacks of Belgium. The corny, sweet and spicy taste is 100% Mexico. Meanwhile, parsnip epitomizes the Ukrainian flavor.

After I discovered and fell in love with this root, my odyssey began: I have been trying out new ways to draw Ukrainian meanings out of parsnip and increase its flavor with various cooking techniques. I baked it for 24 hours, played around with its texture, boiled it with flavorful ingredients. It all came out wrong. Instead of laying bare its Ukrainian soul, I did it all wrong. And then I finally got it. Parsnip should be baked in the oven to increase its sweetness, but not for too long. Bake it for a little while to make it easier to chew; any other actions are a step too far.

That's how cool parsnip is. Anybody who grasps its uniqueness can also grasp the essence of Ukrainian taste.

ON SUGAR BEETS

I want to kneel and thank the universe for giving Ukrainians sugar beets. The stony surface of this root hides perfection. Rude and boorish on the outside, it has a kind soul. It is sweet. It is juicy. It has a cool history. This overlooked hero is 100% Ukrainian.

It took me quite a while to find sugar beets. You can't just buy them in any old shop, but find it I did. Discovering the sugar beet's potential was the next step. I wanted to lay bare its beautiful essence and show it to the world, to improve but not to undermine its taste. That was the hardest.

I found a way. I baked it for 8 hours in a traditional Ukrainian oven, then added salted raspberries, pickled plums, mushroom broth and soft farmer's cheese. This is how it features on the menu of my restaurant, 100 Years Ago Ahead (*100 Rokiv Tomu Vpered* in Ukrainian).

You should eat it slowly, savoring every bite. Take your time to get properly acquainted. Say to it, "Hello, the little sugar beet. You might be strange, but I will try to understand you." Sugar beets are no strangers to Ukrainians; they are a part of our cultural code. They deserve to be more of a presence in the lives of Ukrainians and other nations. I will make every effort to promote them because it helps me to promote Ukraine.

Sugar beet is a bridge between Ukrainian past and future.

#19

ROASTED VEGETABLE PÂTÉ

50 MINUTES   **SERVES 4**

INGREDIENTS:

· 1 ZUCCHINI

· 1 CARROT

· 1 RED BELL PEPPER

· ½ ONION

· 2 CLOVES GARLIC

· 3-4 TBSP. HOME-PRESSED
  SUNFLOWER OIL (CAN BE
  SUBSTITUTED WITH ANY
  VEGETABLE OIL YOU PREFER)

· ½ LEMON

· SALT, PEPPER

1. Preheat oven to 180°C / 350°F degrees.

2. Wash a zucchini, a carrot and a bell pepper well, and pat them dry with a paper towel. Poke the vegetables with a toothpick several times, drizzle with oil and sprinkle with salt. Wrap in foil and bake for 40 minutes.

3. Let the vegetables cool before peeling them. Cut the zucchini, carrot and pepper into slices of any size you like and put them into a blender.

4. Add diced garlic and onion, and blend until smooth. Add oil, salt, pepper and freshly squeezed lemon juice to taste.

5. Serve the vegetable pâté cool.

#20

VEGETABLE SALAD

15 MINUTES   **SERVES 4**

INGREDIENTS:

· 1 ZUCCHINI

· 10 SPRIGS DILL

· 1 TSP. CHILI PEPPER FLAKES

· 1 LEMON

· 10 SPRIGS MINT

· 2 CELERY STALKS

· 2-3 CLOVES GARLIC

· 5 TBSP. VEGETABLE OIL

· SALT, PEPPER

1. Cut the zucchini into thin slices with a peeler.

2. Cut celery stalks into thin slices.

3. Shred green dill manually, and pick leaves off mint sprigs.

4. Carefully mix all ingredients in a bowl.

5. Prepare the dressing. Mix salt, pepper, finely diced garlic and lemon juice with the oil. Add the dressing to the salad and mix carefully.

6. Sprinkle with red chili pepper flakes and serve.

#21

BATTER-FRIED
OYSTER MUSHROOMS

30 MINUTES   **SERVES 4**

INGREDIENTS:

· 400 G / 14 OZ. OYSTER

  MUSHROOMS

· 100 ML / 6½ TBSP.

  VEGETABLE OIL (FOR FRYING)

FOR THE BATTER:

· 240 G / 1½ CUP ALL-PURPOSE

  FLOUR

· 2 EGGS

· 200 ML / SCANT 1 CUP PALE

  ALE OR WHEAT KVASS

FOR THE SAUCE:

· 200 G / SCANT 1 CUP SOUR

  CREAM

· 2-3 CLOVES GARLIC

· FRESH HERBS TO TASTE

  (PARSLEY, DILL)

· SALT, PEPPER

1. Wash oyster mushrooms and split them into smaller segments. Lay them out on an absorbent paper towel to dry.

2. **Prepare the batter.** Season the eggs with salt and pepper to taste and whisk with a fork. Add ale or kvass, then mix again. Add flour and mix until you get the kind of batter you'd use in pancakes.

3. Dip oyster mushrooms into the batter and place on a hot oiled frying pan. Fry until golden brown on all sides.

4. Remove the mushrooms from the pan with a skimmer and place them on a paper towel to remove excess oil.

5. **Prepare the sour cream sauce.** Add finely chopped green dill, parsley and pressed garlic to sour cream. Season with salt and pepper to taste.

6. Serve batter-fried oyster mushrooms with the sour cream sauce.

#22

BAKED PARSNIP

60 MINUTES   **SERVES 2**

INGREDIENTS:

· 4 PARSNIP ROOTS

· SALT

 FOR THE SAUCE:

· 4 TBSP. SOUR CREAM

· 4 PRUNES

1. Preheat oven to 180°C / 350°F degrees.

2. Wash parsnip roots with a brush and peel with a peeler.

3. Give them a generous rub of salt and wrap in foil. Bake for 45–50 minutes.

4. **Prepare the flavorful sour cream sauce.** Add finely diced prunes to sour cream. Mix well.

5. Serve baked parsnips with the sour cream sauce.

#23 TOVCHANKA (POTATO AND BEAN MASH)

60 MINUTES   **SERVES 6**

INGREDIENTS:

- 5-6 POTATOES
- ½ CUP DRIED PEAS
- ½ CUP BEANS
- 3 TBSP. POPPY SEEDS
- 50 G / 3½ TBSP. UNSALTED BUTTER
- SALT AND PEPPER TO TASTE

1. Soak the peas and beans overnight for faster cooking.

2. Cook potatoes, beans and peas in separate pans until ready.

3. Mash potatoes, beans and peas with a potato masher.

4. Season with salt and pepper, add poppy seeds soaked in boiling water, and unsalted butter. Regulate the desired consistency with potato cooking water.

#24

WHITE (OR BLACK) RADISH SALAD WITH SOUR CREAM SAUCE

  |

10 MINUTES | **SERVES 2**

INGREDIENTS:

- 2-3 RADISHES
- 1 TSP. SWEET MUSTARD
- 2-3 TBSP. SOUR CREAM
- 2 TBSP. HOME-PRESSED
  SUNFLOWER OIL (CAN BE
  SUBSTITUTED WITH ANY
  VEGETABLE OIL YOU PREFER)
- 1 TBSP. LEMON JUICE
- 2-3 SPRIGS DILL
- SALT, PEPPER

1. Wash the radishes well and peel them. Grate on the coarse side of the grater or slice into long thin pieces.

2. Add the dressing: home-pressed sunflower oil with mustard, sour cream and lemon juice.

3. Add finely minced dill, mix and season with salt and pepper.

#25

QUICK PICKLED CUCUMBERS IN A PUMPKIN

3 HOURS
(AND 2 DAYS
FOR PICKLING)

SERVES 4-6

INGREDIENTS:

· 1 LARGE PUMPKIN

· 1 KG / 2¼ LB. SMALL

  CUCUMBERS

· 3 TBSP. SALT

· 1 LITER / 4 CUPS WATER

· 5 BLACK PEPPERS

· 5 ALLSPICE BERRIES

· 3-5 BAY LEAVES

· 5-8 CURRANT LEAVES

· 5 CLOVES GARLIC

· 10 SPRIGS DILL

1. Scrub the cucumbers well and soak them in very cold water with ice for 2–3 hours to make them crunchier. Cut off ends and poke with a toothpick to ensure that the cucumbers are pickled all the way through.

2. Wash a large pumpkin well and cut off the top. Remove the seeds and flesh with a spoon to make room for pickles.

3. Fill the pumpkin with cucumbers, dill and currant leaves in layers, add allspice and black pepper, bay leaves and crushed garlic.

4. Dissolve salt in water and pour the brine into the pumpkin so that it covers the cucumbers. Place the cut-off top back in place to cover the pumpkin, and leave it in a cold place for 1–2 days. After the waiting is over, enjoy!

#26

POTATO SAUSAGE

 |

60 MINUTES   **SERVES 4**

INGREDIENTS:

· 6-8 POTATOES

· 150 G / 5 OZ. PORK FAT

· 2-3 ONIONS

· A PINCH OF CRUSHED BAY LEAF

· 3-4 CLOVES GARLIC

· SAUSAGE CASING

· SOUR CREAM FOR SERVING

· SALT, PEPPER

1. Preheat oven to 180°C / 350°F degrees.

2. Boil unpeeled potatoes until ready. Leave them to cool, then peel.

3. Cut pork fat into small cubes and melt on the skillet until soft. In the lard, fry finely diced onions and garlic.

4. Mash or blend the potatoes, add fried pork fat, onions and garlic, season with salt and pepper to taste, add crushed bay leaves and mix well.

5. Fill sausage casings with mashed potatoes to make 12–15 cm / 5–6-inch-long sausages. Poke them with a toothpick several times to make sure that the casings won't break during roasting.

6. Place the sausages on an oiled roasting tray, and cook for 15–20 minutes until golden brown.

7. Serve potato sausages hot with sour cream.

#27 HASH BROWNS BAKED WITH MINCED MEAT

1 HOUR   **SERVES 4**

INGREDIENTS:

- 6-8 POTATOES
- 150 G / 5 OZ. PORK FAT OR FATTY BACON
- 200 G / 1 SCANT CUP SOUR CREAM (AND 1 TBSP. FOR THE DOUGH)
- 2 ONIONS
- 2 EGGS
- 4-5 TBSP. FLOUR
- 350 G / 12 OZ. HOMEMADE MINCED MEAT
- 2 TBSP. TOMATO PASTE
- 5-6 TBSP. VEGETABLE OIL
- SALT, PEPPER

1. Preheat oven to 180°C / 350°F degrees.

2. Grate peeled potatoes on the coarse side of the grater. Add 1 tbsp. sour cream, 1 finely grated onion, eggs, salt, pepper and flour. Mix well and fry hash browns on a hot oiled frying pan until either side is golden brown.

3. On the second frying pan, sweat the cubed pork fat and fry the onion cut into small cubes. Add minced meat and fry it until half-cooked. Add tomato paste, a little bit of water, salt and pepper. Cook for 5 minutes until extra liquid evaporates.

4. Put hash browns and minced meat into a pot in alternating layers. Add 2 tbsp. sour cream to each pot.

5. Bake for 15–20 minutes. Serve with sour cream.

#28

BORENCHYK (POTATO PIE)

1 HOUR | **SERVES 6**

INGREDIENTS:

· 1 KG / 2¼ LB. POTATOES

· 4 TBSP. CORN FLOUR

· 4 TBSP. WHEAT FLOUR

· 3 EGGS

· 150 ML / ⅔ CUP WHIPPING

  CREAM (33%)

· 5 SPRIGS THYME

· 200 G / 1 CUP UNSALTED

  BUTTER

FOR THE SAUCE:

· 3-5 CLOVES GARLIC

· ½ TSP. RED PEPPER

· 1 TSP. SMOKED PAPRIKA

· 1 TSP. PAPRIKA FLAKES

· 1 LEMON

· 1 TBSP. SUGAR

· 2-3 TBSP. TOMATO PASTE

· SALT, PEPPER

1. Preheat oven to 180°C / 350°F degrees.

2. Grate peeled potatoes on the coarse side of the grater. Season with salt and pepper. Add cream, eggs, corn and wheat flour.

3. Grease a ceramic baking tray with butter and dust with corn flour. Fill with potato mass, put 100 g / ½ cup worth of small butter slices on top, and sprinkle with thyme leaves.

4. Bake for 35–40 minutes.

5. Tomato paste. Mix garlic, tomato paste, three types of pepper and a bit of water in a saucepan. Bring to a boil and cook for several minutes, season with salt, sugar, pepper, lemon juice and lemon zest to taste. Blend until smooth.

6. Cut the pie into portion-sized slices. Serve with tomato sauce and melted butter.

APPETIZERS

ABOUT POLTAVA

I have travelled all over Ukraine before reaching Poltava at the very end of my trip. I saved the best for last, so to speak, and it turned that I was hella right. Poltava is a concentrated dose of all things Ukrainian, and a very logical last step for my exploration of the national cuisine. It's not just a regular town: it's the culinary hub of Ukrainian cuisine. During the whole period when Ukrainian identity was under systematic attack, Poltava seemed to have lingered under a protective dome. There was this Ukrainian writer by the name of Ivan Kotliarevsky. A Poltava native and resident, he created the modern Ukrainian literature and encoded dozens of Ukrainian dishes in his 18th-century work *The Aeneid*. He did that so elegantly that the Soviets missed the hint and didn't destroy it the way they used to destroy all things Ukrainian. I wouldn't be too surprised to learn that, since the 1800s to the present, Poltava residents had been reading Kotliarevskyi's *Aeneid* instead of their evening prayers, and cooking traditional Ukrainian dishes first thing in the morning: *shpundra* (meat baked with pickled beets), *halushky* (dumplings without filling), *putria* (a dish of ground barley) and more, all in order to keep the Ukrainian cuisine alive both in their memory and in their lived reality. They were so successful in preserving their Ukrainian identity because they cherished the traditions and the atmosphere that others only knew from books. Yes, Poltava cuisine might not be the most refined; it might be a tad too fatty; their *halushky* are probably not to everyone's taste. Ukrainian cuisine definitely could evolve further, but Poltava has the most important thing: the foundations. And their foundations are a hundred percent Ukrainian. They have even retained the authentic recipes for sugar beet and beetroot kvass, which is quite an achievement. Most importantly, Poltava managed to preserve unique Ukrainian cooking techniques. All you need to do is to take it up and develop it a step further. (Spoilers: this is exactly what I did. I took the basics and developed them to perfection.)

Globally speaking, Poltava residents are foodies as much as the French. They have even installed a monument to *halushky* smack in the town center to admire their culinary heritage 24/7. With a little effort, the amazing Poltava cuisine could beat just about any competitor, hands down. It just needs a little bit of refining and adaptation to contemporary demands, which, it goes without saying, wouldn't change their cuisine's national essence. This mission is wholly possible because Poltava residents have just the right mentality. They cherish, love and cook Ukrainian food. Back in the day, they have even inspired Gogol to write highly evocative descriptions of the national cuisine. Therefore, if you are really serious about reconstructing the Ukrainian national cuisine, you could do worse than to start with Poltava and its take on the matter.

ABOUT ODESA

My relationship with Odesa wasn't love at first sight. Not even at tenth sight. I didn't get what all the fuss was about, I didn't get its jokes, and I didn't like its food; in other words, I didn't understand the first thing about it. I didn't get it until I stumbled into a small courtyard, met an amazing Ukrainian Jewish family, wandered the Pryvoz Market with them, and cooked their borscht. As we sat outside, with the whole courtyard slurping borscht in unison, I finally felt the unique Odesa magic. It didn't matter *what* you were eating, but rather *who* you shared the meal with. Above all else, Odesa residents treasure strong family connections, community spirit and a sense of unity. They aren't quick to welcome strangers into their network of connections, which they take very seriously. At the same time, they also know how to laugh at life, which makes them so charming. Relying on their community, they have created a separate world to which strangers aren't privy. The insouciance with which they flirt with fate had helped them to survive the dark times. Due to all these factors, Odesa, much like Poltava, has kept its traditions and cuisine intact through the ages.

#29

PALIUSHKY (POTATO FINGERS)

60 MINUTES   **SERVES 6**

INGREDIENTS:

- 1 KG / 2¼ LB. POTATOES
- 3 CLOVES GARLIC
- 1 BAY LEAF
- 3 EGG YOLKS
- 160-200 G / 1 CUP ALL-PURPOSE FLOUR
- 1 BUNCH PARSLEY
- 50 G / 3½ TBSP. UNSALTED BUTTER
- SALT, PEPPER TO TASTE

FOR THE SAUCE:

- 5 SPRIGS PARSLEY
- 5 SPRIGS DILL
- 100 ML / 6½ TBSP. WATER
- 100 ML / 6½ TBSP. VEGETABLE OIL
- 50 G / 1¾ OZ. HARD CHEESE
- JUICE OF HALF A LEMON
- 2 CLOVES GARLIC
- SALT, PEPPER

1. Preheat oven to 180°C / 350°F degrees.

2. Cut peeled potatoes into slices of any size. Cover with water and cook with salt, bay leaf and 3 cloves garlic for 15–20 minutes until ready.

3. Drain the cooked potatoes, discard garlic and bay leaf: you'll no longer need them. Mash potatoes until smooth. If you have leftover cooked unpeeled potatoes from the night before, you can also put them through a blender.

4. Add 2 egg yolks, salt, pepper and flour. Mix the dough.

5. Form potato fingers/batons with a spoon or a pastry bag and place them on a baking paper-lined roasting tray.

6. Wash in egg yolk with a silicone brush and bake for 15 minutes until golden brown.

7. **Green sauce.** Put diced green parsley and dill, water, oil, grated hard cheese, lemon juice, garlic and salt in a blender, and blend until smooth.

8. Serve with the green sauce, either hot or cold.

#30

LIVER PÂTÉ

50 MINUTES   **SERVES 4-6**

INGREDIENTS:

· 500 G / 1 LB. CHICKEN LIVER

· 150 ML / ⅔ CUP WHIPPING

  CREAM (33%)

· 70 ML / 5 TBSP. BRANDY

· 100 G / 6½ TBSP. UNSALTED

  BUTTER

· 1 ONION

· 1-2 CLOVES GARLIC

· 2-3 SPRIGS OF THYME

· 2 TBSP. VEGETABLE OIL

· SALT, PEPPER

FOR THE SAUCE:

· 500 G / 1 LB. BLACK CURRANTS

· 250 G / 1¼ CUP SUGAR

· A PINCH OF GROUND BLACK

  PEPPER

· A PINCH OF SALT

1. Fry diced onions and garlic on a mixture of butter and oil. The onion should turn soft and transparent. Afterwards add a sprig of thyme and a pinch of salt.

2. Remove fat and membranes from chicken liver. Put it on the skillet with the onions and fry until ready.

3. Pour in the brandy and give it a couple minutes to evaporate. Turn off the heat and leave the liver to cool.

4. Remove sprigs of thyme and put liver into a blender. Add heavy cream, the rest of butter, pepper and another pinch of salt. Blend until smooth.

5. **Prepare the sauce.** Mix black currants and sugar in a saucepan. Add a little bit of water and boil for 10 minutes. Add a pinch of ground black pepper and salt. Blend until smooth. Serve cool with the currant sauce.

#31 KVASHA (FRUIT-AND-KVASS DESSERT)

 |

25 MINUTES   **SERVES 2–4**

INGREDIENTS:

- 300 ML / 1¼ CUP KVASS
- 100 G / 3½ OZ. SUN-DRIED OR SMOKED PEARS, PRUNES, APRICOTS AND APPLES
- 5 SLICES OF RYE BREAD (ADDITIONAL 150 G / 5 OZ. BREAD FOR THE CHIPS)
- 50 G / ½ CUP WALNUTS
- A PINCH OF GROUND RED PEPPER
- A PINCH OF SALT
- JUICE OF ½ LEMON

1. Preheat oven to 180°C / 350°F degrees.

2. Soak 5 slices of rye bread in kvass for 10 minutes. Add sun-dried or smoked pears and apples (similar to what is used in *uzvar*) to the bread-and-kvass mixture.

3. Bring the mixture to a boil the mixture and leave it to cool fully. Once cooled, remove boiled pears and apples.

4. Either pass the soft rye bread mass through a sieve or pulse in a blender until creamy. Add lemon juice, ground black pepper and salt to taste.

5. Cook rye bread chips. Cut the bread into thin slices and dry in the oven for 3 minutes.

6. Serve *kvasha* sprinkled with finely chopped walnuts. Decorate with rye bread chips.

#32

CHICKEN PUTRIA (GROUND BARLEY PORRIDGE)

1 HOUR | **SERVES 2**

INGREDIENTS:

- 100 G / ½ CUP GROUND BARLEY
- 200 ML / A SCANT CUP HOME-MADE WHEAT KVASS
- 1 CHICKEN BREAST
- 1 CARROT
- 1 ZUCCHINI
- 1 TSP. PAPRIKA
- 1 TBSP. LEMON JUICE
- 1 TBSP. VEGETABLE OIL
- SALT, PEPPER

HOMEMADE MAYONNAISE:

- 1 EGG YOLK
- ½ TSP. SWEET MUSTARD
- 100-150 ML / 6½ TBSP. TO ⅔ CUP VEGETABLE OIL
- 1 TBSP. LEMON JUICE
- SALT, PEPPER

1. Preheat oven to 180°C / 350°F degrees.

2. Soak fine-ground barley in homemade kvass for at least 6–8 hours, preferably overnight.

3. Marinate chicken breast for 10 minutes in salt, pepper, ground paprika, lemon juice and oil.

4. Place chicken breast on a baking paper-lined roasting tray, and cook for 25–30 minutes. It has to be well done.

5. Cut the carrot and the zucchini into very thin slices with a peeler.

6. For the **homemade mayonnaise**, mix egg yolk, mustard, salt and pepper in a bowl, add lemon juice and start whisking. Slowly add the oil at a dribble and mix well until the mayonnaise is smooth and thick.

7. Dress the vegetables with home-made mayonnaise, and put them into individual plates.

8. Put thin slices of the chicken breast and soaked ground barley over the vegetables and serve immediately.

#33

PICKLED MUSHROOMS, APPLES AND ONIONS

 |

15 MINUTES **SERVES 6**

INGREDIENTS:

BUTTON MUSHROOMS:

- 400 G / 14 OZ. BUTTON MUSHROOMS
- 500 ML / 2 CUPS WATER
- 4 TBSP. VINEGAR
- 1 TSP. SUGAR
- 2 BAY LEAVES
- 5 BLACK PEPPERCORNS
- 3 ALLSPICE BERRIES
- 3 SPRIGS DILL
- ½ TSP. CORIANDER SEEDS
- 2-3 CLOVES GARLIC
- ½ ONIONS
- 3 TSP. SALT

APPLES:

- 4 APPLES
- 5 TBSP. SUGAR
- 4 TSP. SALT
- 3 SPRIGS DILL
- 8 BLACK PEPPERCORNS

RED ONIONS:

- 3 RED ONIONS
- 1 TSP. CORIANDER SEEDS
- 2 TSP. SALT
- 8 TBSP. SUGAR
- 500 ML / 2 CUPS WATER
- 5 BLACK PEPPERCORNS

Pickled mushrooms. Wash the mushrooms well and pat dry with a paper towel. Prepare the marinade. Add the following ingredients to 500 ml / 2 cups water: vinegar, sugar, bay leaf, black pepper and allspice berries, finely diced dill, coriander seeds, pressed garlic, salt and onions cut into thin half-circles. Warm the water to help salt and sugar dissolve, and to make sure that the spices release their flavors. Cover the mushrooms with the marinade and leave for at least 1–2 hours.

Pickled apples. Wash apples well and slice into thin slices horizontally. Sprinkle with sugar and salt. Add finely diced dill and pepper berries. Add a little bit of water and leave to marinate for 1 hour.

Pickled red onions. Mix room temperature water with sugar and spice until sugar dissolves fully. Peel the onions and slice into thin circles or semicircles. Cover the sliced onions with the marinade in a small bowl and leave for 1–2 hours.

SOUPS AND BROTHS

ABOUT BORSCHT

Borscht is the first dish I've ever cooked. My father taught me when I was eight. I came back from school one day, and without a word of warning, dad shoved a cabbage at me and solemnly told me that it was time. None too happy with this turn of events, I obediently hacked at the cabbage, and at some point began to enjoy it. My dad and I cooked borscht according to the recipe that is handed down in our family from father to son. That borscht was special. I was brimming with joy and pride, and that's what I have always felt when cooking ever since then.

This is how my cooking history began. For a while, I thought I was the odd one out: nobody in my family is that big on cooking. Most of my relatives treat it like a chore, but eventually I found out that my grandpa was crazy about cooking. Therefore, it wasn't that I was odd: borscht and the love for bringing out various tastes were in my DNA.

By the way, whenever I need a pick-me-up, I think about borscht. You have to take your time and savor borscht, slurp it, and make your enjoyment last. You can eat it with a slice of bacon on a piece of rye bread, or you can chase it with a shot of cold vodka. You can also eat it with onion and garlic, to add a pleasantly sharp tang.

I know that borscht is not just my history. I decided to travel across Ukraine, meet people from every region, and cook borscht with them according to their local recipes. That trip has changed my life. My faith in borscht has grown ever stronger. From a dish that every Ukrainian cooks, borscht has become for me a symbol of the nation's unity. Consider this. We might have different lifestyles, personalities, preferences or views, but one thing unites us all, and that is our love for borscht. If you tell me that the liquid that runs in Ukrainians' veins is blood, I'll just shake my head. Dear friends, it's red borscht that has been coursing in the veins of Ukrainians for ages.

I've tried goose borscht with prunes, cooked from a recipe shared by my artist friends. In Poltava, I tried black borscht with smoked pears and borscht with *halushky*. In the village of Topilche (Ivano-Frankivsk region in the west of the country), I tried the kind of borscht popular with the Hutsul ethnic group: without tomatoes but with *huslianka*, a very cool local fermented milk product. Having tried fish borscht in the village of Vylkove, I finally realized why Shevchenko loved carp borscht. In case you didn't know, Taras Shevchenko wasn't just a Ukrainian poet. He was also a passionate foodie. Give him his oysters, give him his sparkling wine. Contrary to the popular belief, his life wasn't all woe, and those who had been promulgating this idea had bowdlerized the writer's bio. The life of every party, he was fun to be around. After he was released from serfdom, he led a rich life filled with interesting events, people and tastes. It is really no wonder that his menu included carp borscht. In Odesa, a Jewish family shared their recipe of chicken borscht with me. In Uzhhorod, I cooked *bohrach* borscht, with hot peppers and homemade sausages, over an open fire. High up in the mountains, I met Yanko, who treated me to borscht with mushrooms and local herbs, and poured me a shot of his homemade infused vodka (let's skip over the details of the latter). On the border with Belarus, I found a lone house. Its master, the 80-year-old Mykola Pylypovych, preserves the ancient recipe of borscht with sauerkraut and honey. Each of these types of borscht was so delicious it made my hairs stand on end. I've lost count of the times I wept with joy. Incredible taste. Incredible people. Incredible borscht. And it's all ours, Ukrainian.

#34 CHICKEN SOUP WITH HOMEMADE NOODLES

60 MINUTES | **SERVES 6**

INGREDIENTS:

· ½ CHICKEN

· ⅓ CELERY ROOT

· 1 ONION

· 1 HEAD GARLIC

· 1 CARROT

· 2 RED ONIONS

· 2 TBSP. VINEGAR

· 1 TBSP. SUGAR

· 2-3 SPRIGS DILL

· 1 TBSP. VEGETABLE OIL

· SALT, PEPPER TO SEASON THE CHICKEN

FOR THE DOUGH:

· 200 G / 1¼ CUP ALL-PURPOSE FLOUR

· 2 EGGS

· 1 TBSP. VEGETABLE OIL

· 1 TSP. SALT

1. Preheat oven to 220°C / 425°F degrees.

2. Rub chicken with salt, pepper and 1 tbsp. oil. Put it on a roasting tray lined with parchment paper and roast for 20 minutes.

3. Put the roasted chicken in a saucepan, cover with water (2½ liter), and make a broth. Add large chunks of celery, onions, pressed garlic and carrot cut into pieces of any size. Cook for 40 minutes. Add salt to taste.

4. **Dough for homemade noodles.** Combine flour, salt and 1 tbsp. oil. Knead the dough until firm. Leave it to rest in the fridge for 20 minutes.

5. Cut red onions into thin rings and marinate in vinegar with sugar, salt and finely chopped dill. Add a dollop of water.

6. Roll dough thinly and slice into long noodles with a knife. When the soup is almost ready, add the noodles and cook for 1-2 more minutes. The soup is ready.

7. Serve with marinated onions.

#35

VEGAN BORSCHT WITH DUMPLINGS AND BEETROOT KVASS

50 MINUTES   **SERVES 6**

INGREDIENTS:

·¼ CELERY ROOT

·1 ONION

·1 CARROT

·1 BEETROOT

·2 BAY LEAVES

·3 ALLSPICE BERRIES

·2-3 CLOVES GARLIC

·2 LITER / 8 CUPS WATER

·½ WHITE CABBAGE

·3-4 POTATOES

·3-4 TBSP. VEGETABLE OIL

·½ RED BELL PEPPER

·1 CUP TOMATO JUICE

·SALT, PEPPER

FOR THE BEETROOT KVASS:

·0.5 KG / 2.2 LB. BEETROOTS

·200 G / 1 CUP SUGAR

THE DOUGH FOR DUMPLINGS:

·150 G / 1 CUP ALL-PURPOSE FLOUR

·75 G / ⅓ CUP WATER

·1 TBSP. VEGETABLE OIL

·A PINCH OF SALT

1. Prepare beetroot kvass in advance (see the recipe on p. 165).

2. Make the dough for dumplings. Combine all-purpose flour with water, a pinch of salt and 1 tbsp. oil. Knead dough until elastic and no longer sticky. Leave it to rest under a cloth towel or a plastic wrap in a fridge for 20 minutes.

3. Cook vegetable broth. You'll need large chunks of celery root, carrots, garlic and onion, bay leaf, allspice and salt.

4. Cut potatoes into medium-sized cubes and add to the broth. Cook for 10 minutes.

5. Cut the cabbage finely and add to the boiling borscht.

6. Fry the red bell pepper on a skillet for a bit before adding tomato juice. Sautee until it reaches mash consistency, then add to borscht.

7. Form small pieces of dough into dumpling shapes and add to the saucepan with the boiling borscht.

8. After the dumplings begin to float to the surface, pour in beetroot kvass, and add salt and pepper to taste.

#36 VYLKOVE FISH SOUP WITH SALAMUR (MARINADE)

30 MINUTES | **SERVES 6**

INGREDIENTS:

· 1½-2 KG / 3¼-4½ LB. CARP (SILVER CARP)

· 1 RED BELL PEPPER

· 4-5 POTATOES

· 3 LITER WATER

· 2-3 TOMATOES

· 1 PARSLEY ROOT

· 3-5 CLOVES GARLIC

· 2 BAY LEAVES

· 2-3 TBSP. VEGETABLE OIL

· 5 SPRIGS DILL

· 2-3 TBSP. VINEGAR

· 1 SLICE BREAD

· SALT, PEPPER TO TASTE

FOR SALAMUR:

· 1 CUP FISH BROTH

· 5 SPRIGS DILL

· 2 CLOVES GARLIC

· 2-3 TBSP. VINEGAR

1. Scale the fish, remove guts and gills. Wash well and cut into large pieces.

2. Put the fish in a saucepan, cover with water and cook for 10 minutes with parsley root (chopped into large chunks), 2 cloves garlic, bay leaves, and bell pepper cut into small cubes. Season with salt and pepper.

3. Remove 1 cup broth for *salamur* and cool it in a glass jar.

4. Add potatoes diced into medium-sized cubes to the broth. Cook until potatoes are tender.

5. At the very end, add peeled and grated tomatoes. Bring the soup to a boil, cook for 4–5 minutes and switch off the heat. The fish soup is ready.

6. **Salamur.** Add finely chopped dill, pressed garlic and vinegar to the glass jar with cold fish broth.

7. Serve the fish soup hot with *salamur* and a slice of flavorful bread.

#37 BOHRACH (HUNGARIAN STYLE STEW)

90 MINUTES **SERVES 6**

INGREDIENTS:

· 100 G / 3½ OZ. PORK FAT OR
  FATTY BACON

· 600 G / 1⅓ LB. BEEF

· 4-5 POTATOES

· 2 BELL PEPPERS

· 2 TOMATOES

· 1-2 TBSP. TOMATO PASTE

· 1-2 ONIONS

· ½ HOT CHILI PEPPER

· 1-2 TBSP. SMOKED PAPRIKA

· 1-2 TBSP. PAPRIKA

· SALT, PEPPER

1. Cut pork fat into small cubes and render in a deep skillet.

2. Cut beef into bite-sized pieces and fry in the skillet until golden brown on all sides in the pork fat.

3. Cut the onions into 4–8 segments and add to the skillet.

4. Add potatoes cut into pieces of any size to the skillet.

5. Cut tomatoes and bell peppers and add to the skillet.

6. Pour in enough water to cover all ingredients, add tomato paste and stew for 30–40 minutes.

7. Add slices of hot pepper, smoked and regular paprika, salt and pepper to taste.

8. Once cooked, leave bohrach for 20–30 minutes to make it more flavorful. Serve hot.

#38

KHOLODNYK (COLD SOUP)

90 MINUTES **SERVES 4**

INGREDIENTS:

· 2 BEETROOTS

· 300 ML / 1¼ CUPS WATER

· ½ ONION

· 2 TSP. VINEGAR

· 3 SPRIGS PARSLEY

· 3-4 BLACK PEPPERCORNS

· 2 EGGS

FOR MUSHROOM JUICE:

· 150 G / 5 OZ. BUTTON OR
   OYSTER MUSHROOMS

· 500 ML / 2 CUPS COLD WATER

· JUICE OF ½ LEMON

· SALT

1. Preheat oven to 180°C / 350°F degrees.

2. **Button mushroom or oyster mushroom juice.** Cover finely chopped button mushrooms or oyster mushrooms with water, add salt and lemon juice. Blend until smooth and leave for 1–2 hours for more intense flavor and taste. Put the mash through a sieve to get the juice.

3. Wash one beetroot well. Without peeling, bake it for 1 hour.

4. Peel the second beet and grate it on the coarse side of the grater. Cover it with cold water and vinegar, add onion and black pepper, and boil for 15–20 minutes. Before removing from heat, season with salt. Leave the broth to cool fully, then strain.

5. Cook the eggs for 3–4 minutes, then instantly dip into cold water.

6. Peel the baked beetroot and cut it into thin slices.

7. Put the beetroot into a deep bowl, add mushroom juice and beetroot broth. Cut the cooked and peeled eggs in halves and add them to *kholodnyk*. The yolks have to be runny and leak into the soup.

8. Serve garnished with finely diced parsley.

#39

TARATUTA (COLD BEETROOT SOUP)

90 MINUTES   **SERVES 4**

INGREDIENTS:

· 2 FRESH BEETROOTS

· 1-2 GREEN SOUR APPLES

· 1 SMALL ONION

· 500 ML / 2 CUPS BEETROOT
  KVASS

· JUICE OF ½ LEMON FOR THE
  DRESSING (OPTIONAL)

· 2 PICKLED CUCUMBERS WITH
  BRINE

· 1 TBSP. HORSERADISH

· SALT, PEPPER

1. Preheat oven to 180°C / 350°F degrees.

2. Wash the beetroots, pat them dry, wrap them in cooking foil and bake until ready (approximately 1 hour 15 minutes).

3. Peel boiled and cooled beetroots and cut into thin slices.

4. Cut apples and pickled cucumbers into sticks.

5. Cut the onion into thin circles.

6. Mix beetroots with cucumbers and apples, add horseradish and lemon juice, cover with beetroot kvass (for the recipe, see p. 165) and brine from the pickles. Stir well.

7. Season with salt and pepper.

8. Leave it to steep for about an hour in a cool place. Serve cooled.

#40 DUCK NECK SOUP

4 HOURS | **SERVES 4**

INGREDIENTS:

- ½ KG / 1 LB. DUCK NECKS
- 1 DUCK CARCASS OR 300 G / 10½ OZ. BEEF BONES
- 2.5 LITER WATER
- 100 G / 1 SCANT CUP BUCKWHEAT
- 1 ONION
- 1 CARROT
- ¼ CELERY ROOT
- 2-3 CLOVES GARLIC
- 2 BAY LEAVES
- 5 ALLSPICE BERRIES
- 150 ML / ⅔ CUP TOMATO JUICE
- 2 APPLES
- SALT

1. Wash buckwheat well several times under running water and cover with tomato juice and water at the ratio of 1:1. Leave it to soak for 2 hours.

2. In the meantime, cook the duck neck and duck carcass/ beef bone broth. Remove the skin from the necks and cut them into 1.5–2-inch-long pieces. Add the rest of the water, onion, garlic, carrot and celery cut into big chunks of any size.

3. Add 1 apple, cut into quarters, allspice and bay leaves. Cook the broth for 90 minutes. Discard the vegetables (they have already given their flavor to the broth). Add salt to taste. Add soaked buckwheat and cook for 5 more minutes.

4. Cut the second apple into thin slices and fry on a frying pan for 1–2 minutes on each side until soft.

5. You can remove the bones from duck necks, but I like to serve them in portion-sized pieces.

6. Before serving, put several slices of fried apple into each dish.

#41   **GREEN BORSCHT**

1 HOUR   **SERVES 6-8**

INGREDIENTS:

· 2 CHICKEN LEG QUARTERS

· 3 LITER WATER

· 2 ONIONS

· 1 CARROT

· ¼ CELERY ROOT

· 2-3 BAY LEAVES

· 3-4 ALLSPICE BERRIES

· 3-4 POTATOES

· 1 BUNCH SORREL

· 1 BUNCH NETTLE

· 3-4 EGGS

· 3 TBSP. VEGETABLE OIL

· 10 SPRIGS PARSLEY

· SALT

1. Wash the chicken well and pat dry with a paper towel. Cover with water, add a whole onion. Cut half a carrot and a celery root into large chunks, add bay leaf and allspice. Cook over low heat for 30 minutes. Discard the vegetables (they have already released their flavor into the broth, and you won't need them anymore).

2. Cut the second onion into small cubes and fry on a lightly oiled frying pan until soft. Add half of a carrot grated on the coarse side of the grater. Fry everything together for 5 minutes.

3. Cut potatoes into cubes of any size and add to the soup. Cook for 15 minutes.

4. Put eggs in a pan with salted water, bring to a boil and cook for 5 more minutes, then drain and douse with cold water to make peeling easier.

5. A minute before borscht is ready, add chopped greens: half a bunch of sorrel and the nettles.

6. **Green mix.** Cover the remaining sorrel and parsley with 150 ml water (⅔ cup) and blend until smooth. Put it through a sieve and add to the borscht together with the greens. Bring the borscht to a boil, and turn off the heat.

7. Serve hot, adding half a boiled egg to each plate.

#42 KALATUSHA (VEGETABLE AND FISH SOUP)

1 HOUR 20 MINUTES

SERVES 4–6

INGREDIENTS:

FOR THE BROTH:

· 1 CARP OR OTHER SMALL FISH

· 30-40 G / 1-1½ OZ. DRIED PORCINI MUSHROOMS

· 10 SPRIGS PARSLEY

· 5-6 SPRIGS DILL

· 5-6 BLACK PEPPERCORNS

· 2 BAY LEAVES

· 1 CARROT

· 1 ONION

· VEGETABLE OIL

FOR THE SOUP:

· 2 TBSP. ALL-PURPOSE FLOUR

· 2 TBSP. UNSALTED BUTTER

· 3-4 CARROTS

· 1 CELERY ROOT

· SALT, PEPPER

1. Preheat oven to 180°C / 350°F degrees.

2. For the broth, fry carrots and onions cut into pieces of any size on a dry frying pan until they become flavorful and burnt patches begin to appear on the sides.

3. Transfer the vegetables to the saucepan where you'll cook the soup. Pour a little bit of oil onto the frying pan and fry the cleaned fish. Transfer the fish to the saucepan with the vegetables, and cover with 1½ liter / 6 cups water.

4. Add black peppercorns, bay leaf, salt, green parsley and dill. Cook for 40 minutes for intense taste.

5. Strain the broth and put it back in the saucepan. Now add dried porcini mushrooms, and cook for 30 more minutes.

6. In the meantime, prepare **vegetables for the soup**. Peel a celery root and a carrot. Cut them up, sprinkle with salt and oil, and bake for 25–30 minutes until soft. Puree the baked vegetables in a blender.

7. Strain the cooked broth one more time. Put it back in the saucepan, bring to a boil, condense by gradually adding a smooth mixture of 2 tbsp. flour with 2 tbsp. unsalted butter, and carefully stirring with a whisk.

8. To serve, put 1 tbsp. of carrot-and-celery puree into each plate, and carefully cover with the broth. You can decorate it with porcini mushrooms and pieces of boiled fish, removing all bones before serving.

9. Serve hot.

PORRIDGES

ON ROLLED PORRIDGE

I first discovered rolled porridge in the village of Opishnia. You take millet and roll it around in eggs and wheat flour for several hours until each grain of millet gets coated in dough, triples in size and becomes perfectly round.

I'm crazy about this technique. It's so real, so authentic and so Ukrainian that it leaves me speechless. It's the same feeling you get when you see an old friend from a completely new perspective. I picked up a dough-coated grain of millet, took a good look at it, and thought, "That's almost the same technique that Italians use with pasta, but it's ours: our very own and very unique trick."

At the same time, I looked back to my childhood and remembered trying corn sago. I loved that chewy, smooth, round texture in my mouth. And here I am, years later, discovering that we have rolled porridge with the same abso-freaking-lutely amazing texture. Since that trip to Opishnia, I learned even more about Ukrainian cuisine and reached the conclusion that rolled porridge is not exclusive to Poltava region. It's known across eastern Ukraine, Dnipro, Donetsk and Luhansk regions. For me though, it will always be associated with Poltava, because I had discovered it thanks to an ethnographer from Opishnia.

#43 OYSTER MUSHROOM BANOSH

20 MINUTES | **SERVES 2**

INGREDIENTS:

- 100 G / 3½ OZ CORNMEAL
- 210 ML / 1 SCANT CUP MILK
- 85 G / ⅓ CUP SOUR CREAM
- 20 G / ⅔ OZ. HARD BRYNDZA CHEESE (CAN BE SUBSTITUTED WITH SHARP CHEDDAR OR FETA)
- 300 G / 10 OZ. MOZZARELLA
- 1 RED ONION
- 150 G / 5 OZ. OYSTER MUSHROOMS
- 2 TBSP. VEGETABLE OIL
- SALT, PEPPER

1. Fry the cornmeal on a hot dry skillet for 2 minutes.

2. Add milk and cook, stirring constantly, for 2 more minutes. Add sour cream and cook for 1–2 more minutes until ready, seasoning with salt and pepper to taste.

3. Pour a glug of oil onto the second skillet and fry the onion for 2–3 minutes until golden. Add oyster mushrooms, having previously torn them into smaller segments. Fry until all liquid evaporates and mushrooms begin to brown.

4. To serve, sprinkle one layer of hot banosh with grated bryndza (can be substituted with sharp cheddar or feta) and small pieces of mozzarella, and cover with a second layer of banosh and fried oyster mushrooms. Serve hot.

#44

SEMOLINA WITH HEMP OIL

 |

5 MINUTES   **SERVES 2**

INGREDIENTS:

· 100 G / ½ CUP + 1 TBSP. SEMOLINA

· 500 ML / 2 CUPS MILK

· 2 TBSP. HEMP OIL

· 2 TSP. HEMP SEEDS

· SALT, PEPPER

1. Fry semolina on a hot dry skillet until golden and flavorful. Pour in the milk and cook, stirring constantly, for 2–3 minutes until ready and of the desired consistency. Add salt and pepper to taste.

2. Serve for breakfast with a sprinkling of hemp oil and hemp seeds.

#45 KULISH (SAVORY MILLET PORRIDGE) WITH SOUR PICKLED TOMATO AND MOZZARELLA

45 MINUTES | SERVES 6

INGREDIENTS:

- 100 G / 3½ OZ. PORK FAT
- 150 G / ¾ CUP MILLET
- 2 AVERAGE-SIZED MOZZARELLA BALLS
- 1 LITER / 4½ CUPS MILK
- 3 PICKLED TOMATOES
- 3-4 AVERAGE-SIZED POTATOES
- 1-2 ONIONS
- 1-2 BAY LEAVES
- 3-5 ALLSPICE BERRIES
- ¼ CELERY ROOT
- 1 CARROT
- 1 PARSLEY ROOT
- 2-3 CLOVES GARLIC
- 1 LITER / 4½ CUPS WATER
- 3-4 TBSP. VEGETABLE OIL
- GREEN PARSLEY AND DILL TO TASTE
- SALT, PEPPER

1. Cut the pork fat into small cubes of about half an inch (1–1.5 cm). Render it in a cast-iron skillet.

2. Dice the onions, crush the garlic cloves with the flat side of a knife. Add to the skillet with pork fat and fry until translucent.

3. Add carrot, celery root and parsley cut into pieces of any size. Cover with water and milk. Cook the soup for 15 minutes.

4. Add bay leaf and allspice.

5. Peel the potatoes, cut them into pieces of any size, and add to the skillet.

6. Wash and soak the millet in boiling-hot water to make sure that it isn't bitter. Drain the water and add millet to the skillet. Stew everything until ready on low heat for 30 minutes.

7. Season with salt and pepper to taste. Let the skillet rest for several minutes to make *kulish* even more flavorful.

8. To serve, add a sour tomato and a ball of mozzarella to each plate.

9. Serve hot with finely diced parsley and dill (optional).

#46   PUMPKIN PORRIDGE

1 HOUR   **SERVES 4**

INGREDIENTS:

· 500 G / 1 LB. PUMPKIN

· 200 G / 1 CUP MILLET

· 1 LITER / 4½ CUPS MILK

· 1 PINCH OF SALT

· 4 TBSP. SUGAR

· 1 CINNAMON STICK

· 100 G / 7 TBSP. UNSALTED
  BUTTER

· MARIGOLDS (OPTIONAL)

1. Preheat oven to 180°C / 350°F degrees.

2. Peel the pumpkin and cut it into small cubes. Rinse the millet well a couple of times and cover with milk. Add sugar and a pinch of salt.

3. Add pumpkin cubes, half the butter and a cinnamon stick to your millet-and-milk mixture. Cook for 20 minutes over low heat, stirring occasionally.

4. Pour the pumpkin porridge into a cast-iron skillet and add the rest of the butter. Cook in the oven until ready (about 30 minutes).

5. Serve warm. Optionally, you can garnish it with marigold (calendula) flowers to add their unique flavor to the porridge.

#47

TETERIA (MILLET RISOTTO)

30 MINUTES | **SERVES 2-4**

INGREDIENTS:

- 200 G / 1 CUP MILLET
- 100 G / 7 TBSP. UNSALTED BUTTER
- 1 SMALL ONION
- 1 CELERY STALK
- 1 CARROT
- 60 ML / ¼ CUP DRY WHITE WINE
- ½ HOT PEPPER
- 2-3 CLOVES GARLIC
- 30 G / 1 OZ. PARMESAN CHEESE
- 50 G ROLLED BUCKWHEAT
- VEGETABLE OIL

1. Finely dice the onion, celery stalk and carrot.

2. Fry on a skillet with unsalted butter for 2–3 minutes until the onion is translucent.

3. Add millet and pour in dry white wine. Evaporate for 5 minutes.

4. Add slices of hot pepper and minced garlic. Stew with 150-200 ml / ⅔ cup to a scant cup of water for 5–7 minutes. Add the next portion of water and repeat the procedure in 5–7 minutes, the way you would with a risotto. You can replace the water with vegetable or chicken stock (whichever one you like best).

5. To serve, I usually decorate the plate with rolled buckwheat and grated parmesan cheese to balance the textures.

#48

CORNMEAL GRANOLA

 |

45 MINUTES   **SERVES 2-4**

INGREDIENTS:

- 150 G / 1 CUP CORNMEAL
  (POLENTA)
- 60 G / 5 TBSP. SUGAR
- 120 ML / ½ CUP WHIPPING
  CREAM (33%)
- 60 ML / ¼ CUP WATER
- 1-2 TBSP. HONEY FOR SERVING
- 50 G / ½ CUP WALNUTS
- 400 ML / 1⅔ CUPS PLAIN
  YOGHURT
- PINCH OF SALT

1. Preheat oven to 180°C / 350°F degrees.

2. Fry cornmeal on a dry, hot frying pan for 2–3 minutes until it turns golden. Add a pinch of salt to bring out its taste.

3. Add sugar and stir constantly to ensure that the caramel doesn't burn and doesn't melt in large chunks.

4. Wait until cornmeal begins to form caramelized lumps.

5. Add cream and water and keep stirring until you get a uniform mix.

6. Put the mixture on a baking paper-lined baking tray and press down into a layer about an inch thick.

7. Bake in a pre-heated oven for 20–25 minutes until golden brown. Cool thoroughly.

8. Crumble the granola into pieces of any size. Store into a dry glass jar; if hermetically sealed, it can store for up to 1 month.

9. Serve with yoghurt in a bowl.

10. Add your favorite berries, honey and walnuts, and enjoy the splendid taste of a quick breakfast meal while replenishing your vitamins and minerals.

BAKED GOODS

ABOUT BREAD

You should bake your own bread. I'll teach you if you don't know how. If you do, you'll find some new, extra-cool recipes in this chapter. Learning to bake bread is like becoming a magician who can transform water into wine and rocks into gold with a single touch of his fingertips. To learn to bake bread is to get that divine power.

Your relationship with food will reach a new level, more sensual and authentic. You'll love food and know that it loves you back. Bread won't come out delicious unless you love it truly. Baking bread is a highly ritualistic and meditative process: it's all about being in the moment. When you bake, the world disappears in the background, leaving nothing but yourself, your dough and your energy on the center stage. That might sound pompous, but trust me: baking straddles the line between magic and philosophy.

You take the ingredients, mix them and watch the dough come to life and begin to breathe. It plumps up and tries to escape the bowl to be closer to you. You pet it, push it down and soothe it, admiring its perfection. Then you send it into the oven. At this stage, the dough matures and metamorphoses into lovely bread, hot, soft, with a crunchy crust. Making you happy is the meaning of its existence. Making sure that whenever you have a slice, you feel boundless love. The slice of bread you hold in your hands is a fruit of your efforts, brought into the world by your spiritual energy. This is what real bread is all about: it's not about the ingredients and proportions but about love, friendship and authenticity. You can never ever compare it to the bread you can buy in stores.

Bake your own bread. Be empowered. Enjoy.

120

#49

HAMULA (APPLE COOKIES)

90 MINUTES | **SERVES 4**

INGREDIENTS:

FOR THE DOUGH:

· 2 APPLES

· 2 TBSP. SUGAR

· 50 G / 3½ TBSP. UNSALTED BUTTER

· 1 EGG

· 75 G / ¾ CUP OAT FLOUR

· 170 G / 1 CUP + 2 TBSP. ALL-PURPOSE FLOUR

· PINCH OF SALT

FOR THE APPLE MOUSSE:

· 2-3 APPLES

· 3 EGG YOLKS

· 100 ML MILK

· 2 TBSP. SUGAR

1. Wash the apples well. Cut each apple in half and slice out the core. Preheat the oven to 200°C / 400°F. Arrange the apple halves face-down on the foil and bake for approximately 40 minutes or until soft.

2. Remove the skins from the soft cooked apples. The puree will be used both in the dough and in the mousse.

3. **Cookies.** Mix oat and wheat flour, add a pinch of salt and sugar, and mix well. Add unsalted butter and rub ingredients together by hand until you get buttery lumps.

4. Add an egg and 100 g / 3½ oz. of apple puree. Knead dense shortbread dough. Cover it with plastic wrap and leave it in the fridge to rest for 20–30 minutes.

5. Roll out the dough between two sheets of baking paper into a layer 0.5 cm / 0.2 inch thick. Cut out cookie shapes with a glass or a cookie cutter, and place them on a baking paper-lined tray.

6. Bake for 7–10 minutes. Leave the cookies to cool.

7. **Apple mousse.** Mix egg yolks with 225 g / 8 oz. apple puree, milk and sugar in a heatproof bowl. Stirring carefully, heat the bowl with apple mousse for 10 minutes over a pan with simmering water until it thickens slightly.

8. Serve the cookies with cooled apple mousse.

#50

SEMOLINA CAKE

50 MINUTES **SERVES 6**

INGREDIENTS:

· 400 G / 2½ CUP SEMOLINA

· 200 ML / ¾ CUP PLUS 2 TBSP.
  MILK

· 160 G / 5½ OZ. UNSALTED
  BUTTER

· 10 G / 1 TSP. BAKING POWDER

· 250 G /1¼ CUP SUGAR

· 8 EGGS

· POWDERED SUGAR, FOR
  DECORATION

1. Preheat oven to 180°C / 350°F degrees.

2. Separate egg yolks from egg whites. Add half the sugar to egg yolks and mix well with a whisk.

3. Mix semolina with baking powder, add the yolk mass. Mix well.

4. Dissolve butter in warm milk, add the milk mix to the dough. Mix again until smooth and uniform.

5. Beat egg whites with the rest of the sugar until you get soft peaks. Carefully knead it into the dough.

6. Grease the baking form (22–24 cm / 8–10 inches in diameter) with unsalted butter and carefully transfer the dough to it.

7. Bake for 30–40 minutes or until ready.

8. Cool the cooked semolina cake in the baking form to room temperature. Decorate with powdered sugar and serve.

#51

COOKIES WITH POPPY SAUCE

45 MINUTES   **SERVES 6**

INGREDIENTS:

· 200-250 G / 1¼ CUP PLUS
  1 TBSP. TO 2 CUPS FLOUR

· 75 G / 5 TBSP. UNSALTED
  BUTTER

· 100 G / ½ CUP SUGAR

· 1 EGG

· 2 TBSP. SOUR CREAM

· 1 TBSP. POPPY SEEDS

· ½ TSP. BAKING POWDER

· A PINCH OF CUMIN

· A PINCH OF SALT

  FOR THE POPPY SEED SAUCE:

· 100 G / 3½ OZ. POPPY SEEDS

· 250 ML / 1 CUP MILK

· 1 TSP. CINNAMON POWDER

· 2 TBSP. HONEY

1. Preheat oven to 185°C / 365°F degrees.

2. Make the dough. Whisk together the flour, baking powder, a pinch of salt, cumin, poppy seeds and sugar.

3. Add unsalted butter and rub ingredients together by hand until you get buttery lumps.

4. Add egg and sour cream. Knead dough until firm.

5. Roll it out between two sheets of baking parchment into a layer 3 mm / 0.1 inch thick. Poke it with a fork multiple times and bake for 15 minutes until golden.

6. **Prepare the poppy seed sauce.** Mix poppy seeds, milk, cinnamon powder and honey in a saucepan, and simmer for 5–10 minutes.

7. Crumble the cooked flat cake into small pieces and serve in bowls with poppy seed sauce.

8. Serve with hot milk.

#52 BEETROOT BREAD

4 HOURS | **SERVES 4-6**

INGREDIENTS:

- 500 G / 4 CUPS ALL-PURPOSE FLOUR
- 300 ML / 1¼ CUPS WATER
- 10 G / ⅓ OZ. ACTIVE DRY YEAST
- 1 TSP. SUGAR
- ½ TSP. SALT
- 150 G / 5 OZ. BEETROOT
- 100 G / 3½ OZ. BACON
- VEGETABLE OIL (TO GREASE THE BOWL)

1. Wash the beetroot, wrap it in foil and bake at 185°C / 365°F for 60–90 minutes (depending on size). Leave it to cool, then peel and cut into small cubes.

2. Dice the bacon and fry until golden brown.

3. Put flour through a sieve and mix with salt. Dissolve the yeast in warm water, add sugar. Leave it for 15 minutes to give the yeast time to wake up and become active.

4. Add yeast to the mixture of flour with salt, and knead the dough until soft and elastic. Knead in the fried bacon and beetroot cubes. Form a dough ball and carefully move it to an oiled bowl. Leave it in a warm place for 40 minutes until bread rises and doubles or triples in volume.

5. Press down the dough and form a round shape. Place it on a baking paper-lined tray and sprinkle it with flour. Leave for 30 more minutes to rise some more.

6. Bake at 220°C / 425°F for 5 minutes. Then turn the temperature down to 180°C / 350°F and cook for 30 more minutes.

#53

PAMPUSHKY (BUNS) WITH MUSHROOM SAUCE

 |

2 HOURS   **SERVES 4-6**

INGREDIENTS:

FOR PAMPUSHKY (BUNS):

- 500 G / 4 CUPS ALL-PURPOSE FLOUR
- 25 G / 1 OZ. ACTIVE DRY YEAST
- 125 ML / ½ CUP MILK
- 125 ML / ½ CUP WATER
- 1 EGG + 1 EGG YOLK
- 1 TSP. SALT
- 1 TBSP. SUGAR
- 3 TBSP. VEGETABLE OIL

FOR THE SAUCE:

- 400 G / 14 OZ. BUTTON MUSHROOMS
- 1 ONION
- 2-3 TBSP. VEGETABLE OIL
- 200 ML / ¾ CUP PLUS 2 TBSP. HEAVY CREAM (20-30%)
- SALT, PEPPER

1. **Make yeast dough.** Dissolve the yeast in warm water, add sugar. Put flour through a sieve and mix with salt, egg, oil, yeast mixture and water. Knead soft dough. Form a dough ball and leave it in an oiled bowl for 40 minutes.

2. Press down the dough and form small bun shapes. Oil the baking tray and place the buns at a small distance from one another.

3. Leave the buns for 20 minutes for the dough to rise, then brush with egg yolk. Bake at 180°C / 350°F for 20–25 minutes until a shiny golden brown crust forms.

4. **In the meantime, make the mushroom sauce.** Fry finely diced onion on an oiled frying pan for 3–5 minutes, then add sliced button mushrooms and cook until all liquid evaporates. Add heavy cream and simmer for 3 more minutes. Season with salt and pepper to taste. Serve *pampushky* with the sauce.

#54

LEMISHKA (CRISPY FLATBREAD)

45 MINUTES　　　**SERVES 4–6**

INGREDIENTS:

· 120 G / 1 CUP RYE FLOUR

· 300 ML / 3 TBSP. WATER

· 2 CLOVES GARLIC

· 1 TSP. FLAXSEED

· A PINCH OF SALT

1. Preheat oven to 160°C / 325°F degrees.

2. Thoroughly mix the flour with boiling hot water.

3. Add flaxseed, salt and crushed garlic. Mix well. Use a silicone brush to spread the mass across the baking paper in a layer 2–3 mm / approximately 0.1 inch thick.

4. Bake for 25–30 minutes.

5. Leave *lemishka* to cool fully before crumbling it into small pieces. Serve with any dish as a bread substitute.

#55

KUCHERIAVTSI (CRUMBLE CAKE)

 |

50 MINUTES   **SERVES 4-6**

INGREDIENTS:

- 400 G / 2½ CUPS ALL-PURPOSE FLOUR
- 200 G / 7 OZ. UNSALTED BUTTER
- 2 EGG WHITES
- 4 COOKED EGG YOLKS
- 70 ML / SCANT 5 TBSP. WATER
- 100 G / ½ CUP SUGAR
- 100 G / 1 CUP CHOPPED WALNUTS
- 1 TSP. VANILLA SUGAR
- PINCH OF SALT

1. Preheat oven to 200°C / 400°F degrees.

2. Knead the dough. Mix flour with sugar, softened unsalted butter and vanilla sugar. Add cooked egg yolks put through a sieve, finely chopped walnuts, a pinch of salt and water.

3. Roll out ⅔ of the dough on baking paper into a square layer 3–4 mm / approximately 0.1–0.15 inch thick.

4. Beat egg whites to soft peaks and rub the dough with them.

5. Grate the rest of the dough on the coarse side of the grater and evenly sprinkle the egg whites-covered dough with it.

6. Cut into portion-sized squares of 5×5 cm / 2×2 inch with a sharp knife and bake for 20–25 minutes until it turns brown.

7. Optionally, you can sprinkle cooked *kucheriavtsi* with powdered sugar.

#56 APPLE VERTUTA

1 HOUR   **SERVES 4**

INGREDIENTS:

FOR THE DOUGH:
· 300 G / 2 SCANT CUPS ALL-PURPOSE FLOUR
· 100 G / 7 TBSP. VEGETABLE OIL
· 100 ML / 6½ TBSP. WATER
· 1 EGG + 1 EGG YOLK FOR BRUSHING
· ½ TSP. SUGAR
· PINCH OF SALT

FILLING:
· 2 APPLES
· 50-75 G / ⅓ TO ½ CUP RAISINS
· 1 TBSP. CINNAMON POWDER
· 2 TBSP. SUGAR
· 1 LEMON

CREAM GLAZING:
· 200 G / 1¾ CUP POWDERED SUGAR
· 200 G / 7 OZ. CREAM CHEESE
· JUICE ½ LEMON
· 2 TBSP. MILK

1. Sift the flour. Make a well in the flour and add the egg, salt, warm water, oil, and sugar. Knead the dough until soft and elastic.

2. Cover with a linen towel and leave to rest for 40 minutes.

3. In the meantime, prepare the filling. Peel the apples and grate on the coarse side of the grater. Add raisins, lemon juice, cinnamon powder and sugar. Mix well.

4. Roll out the dough in a very thin layer. Cover evenly with the filling and twist into a roll.

5. Put the rolls on the parchment paper-lined baking tray, brush them with egg yolks and bake at 180°C / 350°F for 20 minutes until a shiny golden brown crust forms

6. Once cooked, brush the rolls with the glazing. Whisk cream cheese together with sugar powder, lemon juice and milk until the ingredients are thoroughly blended.

#57

KIFLYKY (ROLLS)

1 HOUR 40 MINUTES

SERVES 6-8

INGREDIENTS:

DOUGH:

· 320 G / 2½ CUPS WHEAT FLOUR

· 260 G / 2 CUPS CORN FLOUR

· 200 G / ¾ CUP PLUS 2 TBSP. UNSALTED BUTTER

· 1 EGG

· 350 G / 1½ CUP SOUR CREAM

· 10 G / ⅓ OZ. ACTIVE DRY YEAST

· 3 TBSP. SUGAR

· PINCH OF SALT

· 1 EGG YOLK, BROWN SUGAR (OPTIONAL)

FILLING:

· 200 ML APRICOT PRESERVE

· 3 TBSP. POPPY SEEDS

· POWDERED SUGAR FOR SERVING

1. Mix flour of both types with cold unsalted butter grated on the coarse side of the grater. Rub the mixture with your hands until buttery crumbles form. Add sugar, salt and eggs.

2. Dissolve the yeast in sour cream and add to the dough. Knead the dough until elastic. Regulate the consistency by adding more sour cream or flour.

3. Wrap the dough in cling film and leave it to rest in the fridge for 1 hour.

4. Take the dough out of the fridge and divide it into two halves. Roll each one out into a layer approximately 20 cm / 8 inches in diameter. Divide it into 6–8 triangular segments. Put the filling (a mixture of apricot preserve with poppy seeds) on the wider side of each segment. Twist into crescent-shaped rolls and put on a baking paper-lined tray at the distance of at least 2 cm / 0.8 inch from one another.

5. Optionally, brush the rolls with egg yolk and sprinkle them with brown sugar. Bake at 400°F / 200°C for 15–20 minutes.

6. Give the baked *kiflyky* a generous sprinkling of powdered sugar.

138

DESSERTS

THE TASTE OF CHILDHOOD

Love needs no reason. It just is. A combination of various factors provokes a chemical reaction in our bodies, causing an addiction with no objective explanation. The same is true of food, especially if that love stems from childhood.

That's the story of my relationship with cherry dumplings. Nobody cooked them better than my grandma. Even at the Dumpling World Championship with experienced grandma contenders, I would still publicly declare that those dumplings that I ate as a child were the best. I used to think that grandma knew some special trick or added a secret ingredient. Once I was old enough to learn that secret, I walked into the kitchen, closed the door firmly

and asked grandma for a recipe for her addictive dumplings. To make sure that nobody overheard our conversation, I even asked her to write the recipe down. Then I cooked the dumplings myself, following the recipe down to a tee, and they still came out wrong. Because it's never about the recipe, you see.

Your memories, the atmosphere, associations, sounds, visuals, emotions, the people around you or, vice versa, your solitude — it all affects your sense of taste. If even one element is missing, love won't happen.

It all happens subconsciously and cannot be explained. If you can pinpoint the reason why you love something, it's no longer love.

#58   LVIV CHEESECAKE

 |

75 MINUTES   **SERVES 6**

INGREDIENTS:

- 0.5 KG / 1 LB. COTTAGE CHEESE
- 2 BOILED POTATOES
- 50 G / 3½ TBSP. UNSALTED BUTTER
- 150 G / ½ CUP SUGAR
- 3 EGGS
- ZEST OF 1 LEMON
- ZEST OF 1 ORANGE
- 50 G / ½ CUP CHOPPED WALNUTS
- 10 G / 2 TSP. VANILLA SUGAR
- 50 G / ⅓ CUP RAISINS
- 1 TBSP. FLOUR
- A PINCH OF SALT

FOR THE CHOCOLATE GLAZE:

- 100 G / 3½ OZ. DARK CHOCOLATE WITH AT LEAST 80% COCOA CONTENT
- 30 G / 2 TBSP. UNSALTED BUTTER
- 80 ML / ⅓ CUP WHIPPING CREAM (33%)

1. Preheat oven to 180°C / 350°F degrees.
2. Make the batter. Mash salt, sugar and vanilla sugar into unsalted butter. Add lemon and orange zest.
3. Separate egg whites from egg yolks.
4. Add egg yolks to the butter mix one at a time, mixing with a whisk after each one until well-blended.
5. Grate boiled potatoes with a fine grater and add to the egg-and-butter mix.
6. Put the cheese through a sieve and add to the mix. Add raisins and knead well.
7. Beat egg whites until stiff and gently fold into the batter.
8. Grease the baking tray with unsalted butter and sprinkle with flour. Gently move the batter into the tray and smooth the surface.
9. Sprinkle the cheesecake with chopped walnuts. Bake for 1 hour.
10. **Make the chocolate glaze.** Mix chopped chocolate with unsalted butter and heavy cream in a heat-resistant bowl. Melt the mixture over boiling water, stirring constantly, until it is well-blended.
11. Pour the chocolate glaze over the cooled cooked cheesecake.

#59

CHEESE KLUSKY (BITES)

 |

20 MINUTES   **SERVES 6**

INGREDIENTS:

- 200 G / 7 OZ. BUCKWHEAT FLOUR
- 720 G / 3 CUPS COTTAGE CHEESE (5% FAT)
- 6 EGGS
- 1 TSP. SALT
- 3 TBSP. SUGAR
- 50 G / 3½ TBSP. UNSALTED BUTTER
- 3 TBSP. HONEY

1. **To make dough for _klusky_**, put cottage cheese through a sieve, add salt and sugar. Blend in the eggs one at a time, mixing them in carefully. Add the buckwheat flour and knead the dough. The exact amount of flour may vary depending on how moist the cheese is.

2. Roll out the dough into a long sausage shape, approximately 1.5 cm / 0.6 inch in diameter. Cut into pieces approximately 3 cm / 1 inch long.

3. Cook _klusky_ in salted water for 2 minutes after they float to the top.

4. Serve with melted unsalted butter and honey.

#60 CREPES WITH NUTS AND SWEETENED CONDENSED MILK

60 MINUTES   **SERVES 6**

INGREDIENTS:

· 520 G / 4 CUPS ALL-PURPOSE

  FLOUR

· 6 EGGS

· 900 ML / 4 SCANT CUPS MILK

· 2 TBSP. VEGETABLE OIL

· 2 TBSP. SUGAR

· 1 TSP. SALT

FOR THE TOPPING:

· 100 G / 1 CUP CHOPPED

  WALNUTS

· 1 TIN OF CARAMELIZED

  SWEETENED CONDENSED MILK

1. Combine eggs, sugar, salt and flour in a bowl. Mix thoroughly until all ingredients are well-blended. Add the milk and mix well once again until smooth, then add the oil and leave the batter to rest for 20 minutes.

2. Fry the crepes on a dry frying pan on both sides until golden brown.

3. Brush each crepe with caramelized sweetened condensed milk and sprinkle with chopped walnuts. Roll the crepes up the way you like them, and serve immediately.

#61

SOUR CHERRY DUMPLINGS

 |

45 MINUTES　　**SERVES 4**

INGREDIENTS:

DOUGH:

- 250 ML / 1 CUP KEFIR OR THIN PLAIN YOGHURT
- 450 G / 3 CUPS ALL-PURPOSE FLOUR
- 0.5 TSP. SALT
- 0.5 TSP. SUGAR
- 0.5 TSP. BAKING SODA
- 1 EGG
- 100 ML / 0.4 CUP SOUR CREAM (FOR SERVING)

FILLING:

- 400 G / 1 LB. SOUR CHERRIES
- 1 TBSP. SEMOLINA
- 2-3 TBSP. SUGAR
- 50 G / 3½ TBSP. UNSALTED BUTTER

1. **Make the dough for the dumplings.** Mix flour with eggs, salt, sugar, kefir or thin plain yoghurt and baking soda. The dough has to be soft, elastic and not sticky. Form a dough ball, move gently to an oiled bowl, and cover with a towel. Leave it to rest for 15–20 minutes.

2. **In the meantime, make the filling.** Pit the cherries (if you are cooking the dumplings out of season, defrost the cherries first). Add 1 tbsp. sugar and semolina.

3. Fold the dumplings by wrapping about a tablespoonful of cherries in a rolled out piece of dough. You can add decorative pleats to the edge when folding the dumpling together.

4. Cook in salted water until the dumplings float to the top. Remove them from boiling water and sprinkle them with sugar to make sure that they don't stick. Drizzle with melted unsalted butter.

5. Serve with sour cream or cherry sauce (*kysil*).

#62 COLD APRICOT SOUP

20 MINUTES   SERVES 2

INGREDIENTS:

· 250 G / 9 OZ. APRICOTS

· 100 ML / 6½ TBSP. WATER

· 70 G / ⅓ CUP SUGAR

FOR THE MILK SAUCE:

· 400 ML / 1⅔ CUPS MILK

· 1 TBSP. SUGAR

· 3 EGG YOLKS

OPTIONAL:

· MINT, HOT PEPPER, DRIED

  NUTS, CINNAMON POWDER,

  VANILLA SUGAR

1. Pit the apricots. Dissolve sugar in water and add pitted apricots. Bring to a boil over medium heat, then puree in a blender until smooth.

2. Whisk or blend the milk, egg yolks and sugar until they are well blended together.

3. Add the milk mixture to the apricot mixture and stir carefully until they are well blended together. Simmer over low heat for 10 minutes, stirring constantly, until the mass begins to thicken.

4. Optionally, you may add cinnamon powder, vanilla sugar, mint, hot pepper or dried nuts.

5. Leave the soup to chill in the fridge for 2–3 hours. It tastes best cold.

LEKVAR (TRANSCARPATHIAN PLUM PRESERVE)

3 HOURS | **SERVES 4-6**

INGREDIENTS:

- 500 G / 1 LB. PLUMS
- 250 G / 1 CUP SUGAR
- 50 G / 1¾ OZ. PRUNES

1. Wash the plums well and pat them dry with a paper towel. Pit the plums and transfer to the saucepan where you will cook the preserve.

2. Add sugar to the pitted plums and leave them for 1-2 hours to let out the juice.

3. Cook for 5 minutes over high heat. Then reduce the heat to medium and cook for 45-50 more minutes until the mixture condenses to the consistency of caramel.

4. Add prunes and puree with a blender until smooth. Put the mass back in the saucepan, bring to a boil again and cook for 5-10 minutes.

5. Pour into sterilized jars and seal. Leave the jars to chill, then store in a cool place.

#64 HOMBOVTSI (PLUM AND CHEESE DESSERT)

45 MINUTES   **SERVES 2**

INGREDIENTS:

· 300 G / 10 OZ. COTTAGE CHEESE

· 1 EGG

· 200 G / 1¼ CUPS ALL-PURPOSE

  FLOUR

· 50 G / 4 TBSP. SUGAR

· PINCH OF SALT

FOR THE FILLING:

· 100 G / ½ CUP SUGAR

· 100 ML / 6½ TBSP. WATER

· 6-8 PLUMS

FOR THE DUSTING:

· 100 G / 1 SCANT CUP

  CORNMEAL

· 50 / 4 TBSP. SUGAR

1. **Cheese dough.** Put cheese through a sieve, add an egg, flour, salt and sugar, and knead the dough. If the cheese is very moist, you might need slightly more flour. The dough has to be dense enough to form cheese balls.

2. **The filling.** Pit the plums and dice them finely. Add sugar and water, then cook for 7–8 minutes until soft. Drain excess syrup: for the filling, you will need only cooked plums without excess liquid.

3. Roll out the cheese dough and put the filling on top. Seal the edges the way you would with a dumpling or pierogi, and form the dough into a round shape.

4. Cook in salted water until *hombovtsi* float. Transfer to a bowl with a strainer and add unsalted butter to make sure they don't stick.

5. **For serving**, I recommend making caramelized cornmeal. Heat the cornmeal on a dry frying pan. Add sugar and fry until the sugar begins to melt and caramelize. Keep stirring until cornmeal begins to stick in lumps, then break them up into small crumbs. Transfer to baking paper and leave to cool.

6. Before serving, sprinkle *hombovtsi* with caramelized cornmeal crumbs.

DRINKS

ABOUT BEETROOT KVASS

Imagine the world in which Ukraine developed with no obstacles. Imagine the world in which nobody tried to erase Ukrainian national identity. Imagine Ukrainians preserving their traditions and enriching them with new knowledge. In this world, every family would have had their own recipe of beetroot kvass: another unique Ukrainian product, another page in our history that was almost wiped out. Ukrainians managed to preserve it though. Beetroot kvass is a fermented drink with a sour, somewhat earthy taste. It breathes new life into things.

Beetroot kvass should run in the veins of Ukrainians instead of blood. My research even helped me to formulate my own theory about the origins of this drink. I think it all started with the Rurik dynasty, the Scandinavians that came to the Ukrainian territories and founded the princely dynasty. It is likely that, at the time, both Scandinavians and Ukrainians knew beetroot. The Ruriks saw a familiar product and decided to make it a smash hit. There was one problem though: the climate. Used to cooler climes, Scandinavians could keep beetroots fresh for months and months. This wasn't an option in our hot summers, so Ukrainians began to ferment beetroots. Therefore, we have been making beetroot kvass since the late 9th century CE, give or take. Imagine the extent of damage to our national memory if our generation, by and large, has never even heard of beetroot kvass.

I want to unlock the memory of beetroot kvass in our cultural code. Make it, drink it, add it to other dishes, and feel centuries of Ukrainian history course through your veins.

#65

VARIANKA (FRUIT VODKA)

 |

5 HOURS   **SERVES 6-8**

INGREDIENTS:

· 200 G / 7 OZ. SUN-DRIED OR
  SMOKED PEARS, PRUNES,
  APRICOTS AND APPLES
· 1 LITER VODKA
· 500 G / 4 CUPS ALL-PURPOSE
  FLOUR
· 300 ML / 1¼ CUPS WARM
  WATER
· SALT
· 1 ROUND BREAD OR ROLL

1. Wash dried fruit under running water and put it into a heatproof ceramic pot. Cover the mixture with vodka and leave the fruit to soak for 30 minutes.

2. Make the dough, mixing flour and warm water with a pinch of salt. Divide it into 2 halves.

3. Seal the pot with the first half of the dough. Cover it with a bread crust or several bread slices before sealing it again with the second half of the dough to ensure that the pot is sealed tight.

4. Put it in the oven at 210°F / 100°C and leave to simmer for 4 hours.

5. Wait for *varianka* to cool and then chill it well.

6. Serve the drink with soaked dry fruit.

#66

SPOTYKACH (MULLED VODKA)

30 MINUTES
(AND ADDITIONAL
10 DAYS
TO INFUSE)

SERVES 6-8

INGREDIENTS:

· 500 ML VODKA

· 6 CLOVES

· A PINCH OF NUTMEG

· 1 TBSP. VANILLA SUGAR

· 100 G / ½ CUP SUGAR

· 100 ML / 6½ TBSP. WATER

· 1 LEMON

1. Put cloves, nutmeg and vanilla sugar into the bottle with vodka. Stir well and leave in a dark place for 7–10 days. Don't forget to stir the mixture every day to make it more flavorful.

2. Make a simple syrup, combining an equal volume of sugar and water. When it's still warm, mix it with the infusion and stir well. Squeeze the juice of half a lemon into the drink, and stir once again.

3. Serve cooled.

#67

MULLED UZVAR (DRIED FRUIT DRINK)

40 MINUTES | **SERVES 6-8**

INGREDIENTS:

· 350 G / 12 OZ. SUN-DRIED OR
  SMOKED PEARS, PRUNES,
  APRICOTS AND APPLES
· 3 L / 12 CUPS WATER
· 7-8 TBSP. HONEY
· 3 CLOVES
· 1 TBSP. POPPY SEEDS

1. Wash dried fruit well in a skimmer under running water. Cover with water and simmer over low heat for 30 minutes with the lid on to make the taste more intense.

2. Turn off the heat, add cloves and poppy seeds. Mix well and leave to cool.

3. While *uzvar* is still warm, add honey to taste.

4. Cool well and serve.

162

#68

BEETROOT KVASS

 |

**15 MINUTES
(AND 4 DAYS
TO FERMENT)**

SERVES 6

INGREDIENTS:

· 1 KG / 2¼ LB. BEETROOT

· 400 G / 2 CUPS SUGAR

· WATER

1. This is a quick way to make kvass using a lot of sugar. If you want to make this kvass with less sugar, you will need more time (up to 7–10 days) to ferment. Check the readiness of kvass to taste.

2. Wash the beets well and peel them. Dice them finely and put into a 3-liter / 3 quart glass jar. Beetroots will take up approximately 2/3 of its volume.

3. Add sugar and cooled distilled water to a level 3–5 cm / 1–2 inches above the beetroots.

4. The jug has to have room for kvass to ferment. When bubbles appear on the surface, it's a sign that the fermentation process is underway.

5. Cover the jar with a cheesecloth folded in 4 layers, and leave it in a warm place for 3–4 days.

6. Once the kvass is ready, store it in the fridge.

#69

HONEY KVASS

**10 MINUTES
(AND 5 DAYS
TO FERMENT)**

SERVES 4

INGREDIENTS:

· 300 G / 10 OZ. HONEY

· 1 L / 4 CUPS WATER

1. Dissolve the honey in warm distilled water. Pour into a glass jar and cover with a cheesecloth folded in 4 layers. Leave in a warm dark place for 5–6 days to ferment.

2. By the end of that period, the fermentation process should be completed. You can seal the jar tightly with a lid and store it in the fridge.

3. Serve this non-alcoholic beverage cooled. Optionally, you can add sparkling water and enjoy the taste.

#70

BERRY KYSIL (STARCH DRINK)

20 MINUTES   **SERVES 6-8**

INGREDIENTS:

· 400 G / 14 OZ. OF
   BLACKCURRANTS,
   REDCURRANTS, CHERRIES AND
   STRAWBERRIES
· 10 TBSP. SUGAR
· 2½-3 LITER / 2½-3 QUART
   WATER
· 5 TBSP. STARCH

1. Bring water to a boil in a saucepan and add sugar (it has to dissolve fully). Add a mixture of your favorite fruit and berries. Cook for 5–10 minutes to infuse the water with their taste.

2. Dissolve starch in a glass of cold water and gradually add to the fruit mixture, stirring constantly to avoid the formation of starch clots.

3. Cook for several more minutes until the *kysil* thickens.

4. Serve *kysil* well cooled.

HOW THE SOVIET CUISINE CAME TO REPLACE
AND DISPLACE THE UKRAINIAN CUISINE

When I was pursuing a degree in international finance, I did a lot of travelling abroad and researched how different countries interacted and influenced one another. When I switched to culinary arts and began working with various national cuisines, I already had a basic map of global relations in my head. Whenever I encountered a new product or dish, I automatically mapped its relations to various countries: how Chinese cuisine came to Italy and the UK, changing in the process; how and where forks first appeared, etc., etc. Much like a language, cuisine is always in flux as it migrates from one region to the next. We are enriched with new products and cooking techniques adopted from other traditions, much like our language is enriched with loan words.

As a child, I was suspicious of the dishes that everybody used to cook. The traditional holiday food for the New Year season was especially unappetizing. As a young boy, I expressed my opinion of this festive cuisine as "ew, yuck." Once I grew up, I tried to make sense of my feelings. I went to a culinary school in Paris and finally figured out why I had distrusted Soviet cuisine. The French had similar dishes, but with a different meaning and different cooking principles. For example, let's take aspic, which we eat as a meat jelly. The French cook aspic too, not as a standalone dish, but as a sauce thickener. When I told French chefs that we eat meat jelly as a standalone dish, they thought I was crazy. I became the butt of all jokes. Later

I found out that vinaigrette, a beloved salad in all former USSR countries, is one of the five basic French sauces, its name deriving from the French word for vinegar. I have no idea why we use the word to describe a salad of beetroot, potatoes, carrots, pickles and sauerkraut. Mayonnaise? Yup, that's a basic French sauce too. The French have a fairly elegant approach to eating it, whereas in the Soviet Union, people used to smother all salads with mayo. Mix boiled potatoes and carrots with sausage or canned and/or salted fish, add mayo, and you have all salads in the Soviet Union: oodles of mayonnaise over boiled vegetables. Never mind the difference in taste between the French mayonnaise and what was known under this name in the USSR. The famous Soviet salad "Mimosa" (boiled potatoes, carrots, eggs, fresh onion, canned fish and the inevitable mayo) is a bastardized version of the eponymous French dish. The French "Mimosa" is a kind of devilled eggs. The French have sautés too, but they use ingredients like celery roots, whereas in the Soviet Union it was a different story altogether. Not a single interesting taste: just oil, carrots and onions.

To sum up, the Soviets took the French cuisine, stripped it of its taste and meanings, and based the Soviet meal plan on these bastardized foundations. Food for the working class: let them stuff their faces and not think about it too much. Sounds plausible? Absolutely. The Russian Empire was friends with France. French chefs lived and worked on the territory that later became the Soviet Union. The new regime took their culinary know-how, simplified it, cheapened it to make it more accessible to the poor controllable population, and handed it down to the people. These bastardized dishes were first cooked in factory canteens; having tried them, the workers brought that meal plan back home with them. The food for the masses, neither nutritious nor delicious, is what we inherited from the Soviet days. For whatever reason, we keep reproducing it with loving care.

Under the circumstances, Ukrainian cuisine didn't stand a chance. Propaganda, food shortages and outright prohibitions made short work of it. Also, authoritarianism, dictatorship and fear. Our language, literature, traditions and church were all banned, and so was our cuisine. Our books were being destroyed, our material heritage was being shipped abroad. The oppressor's logic was simple: if you want to conquer and remake a nation, take away its food. It's nothing short of a miracle that Ukrainians managed to save several cookbooks and the genetic knowledge of their identity through centuries of oppression. This is evidence that Ukrainians have a strong backbone. If not for it, I wouldn't have found the forgotten recipes, wouldn't have revived them and showed these discoveries to Ukrainians and the world. We have *The Aeneid* by Ivan Kotliarevskyi, an epic poem with long lists of Ukrainian dishes. The names of national dishes hidden in last names and place names by our ancestors had helped us to keep an unbroken connection to our past. Our ears are still familiar with the words *putria*, *shpundra* and *vereshchaka*. The Soviet regime had tried to rob us of our traditions, but we have proven that authentic and integral symbols inscribed in the heart of the nation can never be destroyed.

INDEX:

WE BELIEVE THAT
LOVE IS THE BEST GIFT.

To love yourself is to make time just for yourself. To love your children is to want them to grow up in a world without borders and boundaries, believing in miracles and knowing that they the sky's the limit. To love your near and dear is to want to share not just a few experiences but the whole world with them.

We are committed to publishing the books worthy of love: the books that tell spellbinding stories, inspiring the readers to dream and learn; the books that reveal the vibrant world, sweeping perspectives and endless opportunities; the books that become an expression of love when you share them.

We are happy that you are holding this book. We know that #knigolove is the best gift because #knigolove is love, and love begets love.

#knigolove